The Life of a Crazy Japanese Immigrant

~ A Memoir

MASAYUKI OHKUBO

FOREWORD BY KRISTINE OHKUBO

Copyright © 2023 by Masayuki Ohkubo.

All rights reserved. No part of this publication may be reproduced, distributed, or transmitted in any form or by any means, including photocopying, recording, or other electronic or mechanical methods, without the prior written permission of the author, except in the case of brief quotations embodied in critical reviews and certain other noncommercial uses permitted by copyright law. For permission requests, contact the author using the webpage address provided below.

https://masayukiohkubo.wixsite.com/author

The Life of a Crazy Japanese Immigrant/Masayuki Ohkubo. —1st ed.

ISBN: 978-1-0880-8867-8

All persons mentioned in this book are real people; there are no composite or fictional characters. The names of some individuals have been changed to respect their privacy.

Foreword

Cultural generalizations and stereotypes—no country is immune to them, particularly Japan. According to one source, "Japan has the unfortunate honor of being one of the most stereotyped nations on Earth."[1] In the eyes of countless foreigners, Japanese people are typically seen as shy or quiet, especially when traveling abroad. However, shy and quiet are not the adjectives one would use to describe **Masayuki Ohkubo**. Whether you were recently introduced to Masayuki or have known him for many decades, the words which come to mind when describing him are gregarious, mouthy, jocular, and unconventional.

Masayuki (Mickey) Ohkubo was born in a rural town in Nagano Prefecture on March 11, 1952, just a few weeks shy of the conclusion of the Allied Occupation of Japan. The Allies occupied the country after the *Japanese Instrument of Surrender* was signed on September 2, 1945, until the *Treaty of San Francisco* took effect on April 28, 1952. By the end of 1945, approximately 430,000 American soldiers were stationed throughout the country.[2]

Japan's Westernization began during the occupation and continued during the postwar era. American music and movies were popular and produced a generation of Japanese entertainers who built on Western and Japanese influences. Overall, Japanese people tended to associate the luxury and convenience of American life with progress.

---

[1] Afshar, Dave. "Stereotypes All Japanese People Hate." The Culture Trip, 23 Jan. 2017, https://theculturetrip.com/asia/japan/articles/15-stereotypes-all-japanese-people-hate/.
[2] "Occupation of Japan." Wikipedia, Wikimedia Foundation, 17 Mar. 2023, https://en.wikipedia.org/wiki/Occupation_of_Japan.

Growing up in post-war Japan, Masayuki witnessed both the damaging consequences of war and the excesses of American culture. As a young, impressionable boy, he watched in awe the Hollywood films depicting Americans living in luxurious homes, wearing nice clothes, eating sumptuous meals, and driving expensive cars. Unsurprisingly, he grew envious of the American lifestyle. When tragedy struck in 1964, Masayuki suddenly found the trajectory of his life altered and became rebellious.

In 1971, a fortunate invitation from a couple in California, enabled him to experience the wealthy American lifestyle firsthand in Berkeley. The seed of going to school in the U.S. took root in Masayuki's thoughts, and he soon became obsessed with the idea. After returning to Japan, he did everything imaginable to realize his ambition.

Masayuki succeeded in his mission to study in America and graduated from one of the most selective schools in the country, which accepts only 30.2 percent of the students applying to it. With a degree in hand and his fiancée by his side, he returned to Nagano to fulfill his filial duties. But nothing in Masayuki's early life ever took a standard turn. Joni, then the love of his life, returned to America, with Masayuki pursuing her close behind. What transpired afterward forms most of the basis for *The Life of a Crazy Japanese Immigrant*.

At times, Masayuki's experiences were heart-breaking. At other times, they were enormously funny. These stories will make you laugh hysterically, cry, and ask yourself, "Was the younger version of me ever this crazy?"

I believe you will find these stories both relatable and enjoyable.

—Kristine Ohkubo
Author

i. Masayuki Ohkubo, Nagano, Japan

Table of Contents

Foreword i
Preface 1

Nagano 3
Saitama 39
Return to Nagano 71
Stockton 85
Modesto 103
San Luis Obispo 125
Nagano Homecoming 139
Back in the U.S.A. 145
Los Angeles 185
Appendices 293

    Appendix A Links to My YouTube Channel 294
    Appendix B Cars I Owned 295
    Appendix C Photos 296

Works Cited 298

Preface

At the time of this book's publication, I will have reached the ripe old age of seventy-one. It is a good age to recall and reflect on the experiences that have helped me reach this juncture in my life. Although I had related some of my experiences about growing up in postwar Japan to my wife, author Kristine Ohkubo, for her book *The Sun Will Rise Again* (2017), there were many more stories that remained untold. Many of them are reflected in the photographs that fill several boxes in my closet. Sometimes, I look through the photos, recalling the people and places in this life of seventy-one years. On occasion, I share some of the more memorable stories with my wife, family, and friends.

During one such occasion, my wife suggested I write a book about my experiences. At first, I was a little apprehensive about taking on such a monumental task, but after giving the matter further thought, I decided to follow through on it.

Even though every life lived is a story worth telling, I believe that my life is unique. It is unusual as I have done things that other people only briefly imagine doing, and it consists of actions that other people would not even have dared to dream of doing. Hence the title, *The Life of a Crazy Japanese Immigrant*.

The distinguished American actor and comedian Danny Kaye once said, "Life is a great big canvas, and you should throw all the paint on it you can," and I have. Mine is a life well-lived, and every speck of canvas has splatters of paint on it. Some colors are vibrant and bright while others are dark and dismal. The stories I will share with you represent the various shades of paint which decorate my life's canvas.

Just as people perceive the same work of art in different ways based on their own perspectives and experiences, I think each and every reader will interpret my life's story in their own unique way. Regardless of what you take away from reading this book, I hope these stories will enlighten and entertain you.

—Masayuki Ohkubo
August 20, 2023
Los Angeles, California

Nagano

This Is No Ordinary Family

My name is Masayuki Ohkubo; people call me Mickey. I was born on March 11, 1952, in the town of Shinonoi in Nagano Prefecture, Japan. The town was home to approximately 25,000 people. Shinonoi merged with several towns and villages in 1966, creating the city of Nagano.

I currently live in Redondo Beach, a suburb of Los Angeles. I am 5'7" tall and weigh 162 pounds, but when I was in school, I was always grouped with the smaller kids. I suppose you could say I was a small kid from a small town, but don't let that fool you. I was always active, friendly, inventive, talkative, energetic, stubborn, and hard-working whenever my mother asked me to help her.

At the age of thirty, I learned a long-kept secret from my mother. She confessed that she never liked my name. This was because her mother-in-law had asked a Buddhist nun to name me without my mother's consent. These days, when people call me on the phone and ask if I am Masayuki, I respond by saying, "It sounds like my ugly name." The callers are often surprised to learn that I do not like my name. I have to respect my mother's opinion.

My Brother

I had a brother who was two years older than I, named Yukio. Yukio was an easy-going guy who never excelled in school. He had reddish hair, so his friends nicknamed him *Meriken* (American).

Even though we fought, we usually got along fine and did a lot of things together. Once, during a fight, he threw a rock at the back of my head. It hit me so hard that it cut my skin open and I bled a lot. To this day, I still have a scar there.

Whenever other kids picked on Yukio, I always came to his rescue, regardless of how tall or how much older the person picking on him happened to be. My brother and I loved each other very much.

Unfortunately, he died in a tragic accident when he was just thirteen years old. It has been almost sixty years since he passed away, and I still miss him dearly.

My Father

My father's name was Takeshi. He was one of four children, three boys and one girl, born to a wealthy farming family who owned a substantial amount of land. He was slightly taller than I am. At that time, about 85 years ago, he was considered rather tall for a Japanese man. My uncles were even taller than my father.

After graduating from Matsushiro High School, my father went to Tokyo in search of work and became a part-time boxer. He was a handsome man with a muscular build. He returned to Nagano after a few years to help his parents grow rice and apples.

In Imperial Japan, all able-bodied men aged 17 to 40 were drafted for a period of three years. My father managed to avoid being drafted for the Pacific War after claiming that he had a bad knee. Whether this was true or a sham, I will never know.

My father was thirty years old when he married my mother. She was three years his junior. My grandparents gifted them a new two-story house very close to their home.

My mother later told me that when my parents were newlyweds, my father regularly returned home late at night after spending time with his parents and friends. She was scared to stay home alone at night, because she constantly heard cracking noises coming from the newly constructed wooden house. I think it took my father some time to mellow out and get used to married life. My mother also mentioned that she was the only person who was capable of putting up with my father's waywardness. She later declared, "Your father really liked me because I was very cute!"

He owned a truck and worked as a truck driver until the age of sixty-eight. He purchased a new truck every five years or so, and he performed all the maintenance work on his vehicles.

He got up at 3 a.m., without exception, and went to the Shinonoi train station. There, he picked up bundles of newspapers and brought them to the distribution center in the next town. He returned home within an hour and went back to sleep, only to wake up again at 6 a.m. As soon as he finished his breakfast, he left the house in his truck and drove to the various milk collection facilities, about ten in all, to pick up containers of milk that weighed nearly sixty pounds each. He collected up to fifty containers on any given day and brought them to the Meiji milk processing center in Nagano City. Then he came back home around noon, ate his lunch, and took his usual one-hour nap. He seldom helped my mother with her farming work. In his entire career, my father took only two days off from work, and that was when my brother died. My father passed away from heart disease at the age of seventy-six.

My Father's Parents

I do not remember much about my grandparents, although I do recall being babysat by my grandfather on occasion. One memory that sticks out in my mind was when my grandfather sneezed and his dentures flew out of his mouth.

My grandmother was a relatively tyrannical woman. I believe she arranged all four of my father's marriages. My father's first wife died soon after they were married. His second wife was pregnant with another man's child before she married my father. When my grandmother found out, she kicked that wife out. Grandmother did not get along with the third wife and kicked her out as well. Then came my mother, my father's fourth wife.

My Mother

My mother's name was Seki. She was the second youngest of five daughters born to a couple who initially managed quite well as rice growers. However, my grandfather loved to invest in commodities and antique goods. This plunged the family into poverty.

My mother only attended school through the third grade, then she began helping her parents with their farming. She was 20 years old when the United States declared war on Japan, following the attack on Pearl Harbor. She found a job at a cotton mill in Nagoya City in Aichi Prefecture and said good-bye to Nagano, albeit only briefly.

She later found work in Tokyo as a maid, employed by an executive of what was to become Toshiba Corporation. Unfortunately, the job had only lasted for six months when she was relieved of her duties. Although the family she worked for was financially well off at the time, they could not afford to feed everyone in the household due to wartime food shortages. My mother left Tokyo and returned to Nagano, where she found work in a blacksmith shop. She worked there until 1949, the year she married my father.

After she married, my mother focused on farming and grew rice, wheat, apples, and peaches. She was an extremely hard-working person, and she was always on the go. Even in her late eighties, she walked much faster than my wife and I could. She worked at least 12 hours a day except during the winter months. She accomplished every task with speed and efficiency, and she maintained this pace until she retired at the age of eighty-eight.

At the age of fifty-two, my mother found work at a small local company as a press operator to earn more money for my education in the U.S. She worked there from 8:00 a.m. to 5:00 p.m., five days a week, and she was very well-liked by the owner for her speed and efficiency. Before starting her job and after returning home, she tended to her apple and peach orchards for a total of four hours. When she no longer needed to send me money, mother returned to her life as a farmer and grew apples and peaches.

My mother was extremely picky about everything that she produced. She had twenty apple trees occupying half an acre of land. When the trees were fully grown, the diameters of their trunks exceeded one and a half feet each and they reached a height of fifteen feet. My mother did not tolerate any weeds growing in her orchards. She was constantly pulling weeds by hand, and she often enlisted my brother and me to help her. She refused to use chemicals to kill the weeds. She really worked hard to take care of her apple orchard.

I remember that when I was a child, my mother's apples fetched a much higher price than the neighbors' crops did. For the entire harvest, she earned $10,000. Sixty years ago, that was a pretty good amount of money.

From the end of November to the end of February, she took time to rest and recharge. In mid-March she hired someone to prune the apple trees, and she scraped the old bark from the tree trunks to make certain that insects did not dwell underneath them. She basically repeated the same process with her peach trees. Her attention to detail allowed her to grow good quality vegetables as well.

My mother was a very conservative person with traditional values. She did not want me to experience the poverty that was part of her youth, and she encouraged me to find a job with the local government. Even though local government jobs did not pay well, they afforded steady employment. To my mother, stability and security were of utmost importance. However, I turned out to be a rebellious and different, or unique, individual.

About six months prior to her passing, my mother suffered from aspiration brought on by food entering her lungs. It lead to pneumonia. In the last three months of her life, she was unable to eat and was placed on an IV. Sadly, I was unable to be by my mother's bedside when she died at the age of ninety-four. Unlike what happened with my father, I did take a few opportunities to express my gratitude and thanked her for taking care of me and helping me.

Passing Gas

One evening when I was in 5th grade, we were all gathered in the living room watching TV. Then, all of a sudden, my father stood up and said, "Yes, I am coming." He started walking toward the front door. We heard him open and close the front door, after which he returned to the living room with a puzzled look on his face. He mumbled, "It is really strange. No one was at the door." When my mother saw him walking back to the living room, she had a mischievous grin on her face. As he sat down, she said, "You mistook my passing gas for a knock on the door!"

Elementary School Years (Grades One to Six)

My parents were very busy, so I was enrolled in preschool at the age of three. Afterward, I attended kindergarten until I was five years old.

Fortunately, my elementary school was next door to my kindergarten, so I was very familiar with the area. I had a total of three homeroom teachers, one from first through third grades, one in the fourth grade, and another in the fifth and sixth grades.

ii. My father, Takeshi

iii. My mother, Seki, my older brother, Yukio, and me

School Lunch

Lunch was my favorite time of the school day. The school provided lunch to the students free of charge; serving lunch was a duty that students were expected to perform. In-house dieticians cooked our lunches in the school kitchen. The students took turns bringing the meals to the classrooms and serving them to the other students. After eating lunch, we brought the bowls, plates, cups, and dirty utensils back to the kitchen.

The Winter Months

Winter in Nagano can be brutally cold. In early November, our parents set up a coal-burning stove in each classroom. As fourth graders, our chores included maintaining these stoves. We arrived early in the morning, removed the ashes from the previous day, and got the stove going for the remainder of the school day.

Since our school buildings were quite old, a coal-burning stove was not sufficient to keep the entire classroom warm. We often had to wear many layers of clothing to keep ourselves warm during the winter months.

No Way to Impress a Lady

I endured one of the most embarrassing moments of my life in the third grade. There was a very cute girl in my class with whom I was completely infatuated. Normally, my business in the school bathroom did not involve "number two," but on this particular day, I had no choice.

There are two styles of toilets commonly found in Japan. The oldest type is the *washiki* (a simple squat toilet), which is still common in some public places. After World War II, modern Western-type flush toilets and urinals became more common.

So, there I was, squatting in the toilet and taking care of business when someone knocked on the door. Thinking that I had locked the door, I simply ignored the knocking. The next moment, the door was flung open and there stood the cute girl I liked. She was standing there looking down on me when our eyes met. I was speechless and did not know what to do.

Fortunately, she simply closed the door and walked away. Up until that moment, the only other person who had seen my naked derriere was my mother. It was both awkward and agonizing to return to the classroom afterward. To this day, I feel that it was one of the biggest mistakes of my life.

Cleaning the Washiki

It took some time for the modern Western-type flush toilets to become common in Nagano. The washiki basically consisted of a deep hole where we deposited our business. As such, it had to be emptied every two months. This unpleasant task was carried out by my father.

Armed with a large, two-quart ladle attached to a four-foot pole and two seven-gallon buckets, my father completed the task. He scooped the contents of the washiki into the two buckets and covered them with bundles of dried rice plants. This prevented the contents from spilling over. Using their rope handles, he attached each bucket to a yoke and carefully carried the waste out on his shoulders. Since we lived in rural Nagano, it is not difficult to imagine what became of the waste once it was scooped out of the washiki. My father dumped the contents of the buckets into a large storage tank buried in the ground. The waste remained there for two years, after which it was used to fertilize my mother's fruit trees. My father handled that task as well. He spread the aged waste in a circular pattern around my mother's apple trees and carefully placed it at least five feet away from the trunks; otherwise, the apple trees might have died.

Falling Into a Holding Tank

When I was growing up, waste holding tanks were quite common in rural Nagano, but that did not mean we were always aware of them. A rice grower had placed a waste holding tank in a corner of his rice field. Unfortunately, the tank had a very flimsy cover on it. The way it looked, no one would have guessed that it hid a waste holding tank.

One day, as I was playing with my friends, I accidentally stepped on that flimsy lid. My right foot broke through, and I soon found myself immersed up to my hip in nasty waste. I did what any country boy would do; I jumped into the nearby river to clean myself off. As you read on, you will find that I have had a deep and profound relationship with human waste.

Scarcity Is the Mother of Invention

Due to the effects of World War II, food was scarce in Japan for a number of years. But since my mother grew rice and vegetables, we were pretty self-sufficient. Our diet consisted mainly of rice, vegetables, and fish, although we occasionally ate meat, which happened to be my father's favorite food.

My parents worked hard. As a result, we were much better off than most other people in our village. My mother and father ensured that we always had the basic necessities, but they did not believe in spending money on things that they considered extravagant.

These days, whenever I see kids on TV being picky about what they eat, or when they are given any toy they desire for Christmas, I tell my wife, "These kids are spoiled. I was born after World War II, and my brother and I had to make our own toys and forage for snacks to eat."

It isn't an exaggeration. When my brother and I wanted something to snack on, we searched for the nests of honey wasps under the eaves of houses. It wasn't the stored nectar we were after but the wasp larvae. The baby wasps resemble small worms or grubs. We fried them in oil and ate them for snacks.

Sometimes, we found the white larvae of a different insect in the pile of branches from my mother's apple trees. My mother placed the cut branches in a certain spot under the roof, and within four to five years, larvae up to two inches in length lived among the branches. While the larvae were busy feasting on the branches, we picked them out, cooked them, and ate them the same way we ate the wasp larvae. We had to be careful while we were frying the big ones, as they often exploded in the hot cooking oil. In those lean years, the larvae were a good source of protein for us.

Our favorite snack was the potatoes my mother grew in the field behind our house. My brother and I dug them up, boiled them, and ate them with a little salt.

Toys were considered an extravagance, so our parents never bought us any. That did not stop my brother and I from making our own toys. It is true when people say that scarcity is the mother of invention. I was very resourceful and made a variety of toys with which to entertain myself. I once made a go-cart that did not have an engine. My friends pushed the cart from behind with me in it.

Over the years, my creations included a bow and arrow, a bow gun, various Japanese swords made from willow branches, and an air gun fashioned from a radio antenna and a bicycle tire pump. I also made a handgun from the stem of a truck tire, air rifle bullets, and the carefully collected powder from fire crackers.

I was creative, but that did not mean that my creations were safe. Once, when I fired the hand gun I had made, it exploded in my hand. Luckily, I was wearing a glove and did not sustain any damage.

The Missing Person

As a third grader, I suffered from middle ear disease. One snowy Saturday morning, my father dropped me off at my otolaryngologist's office, located approximately seven miles from our house. He told me that he would return to pick me up at a certain time after finishing his errands. My father was usually a very punctual man, and when he did not show up at the promised time, I began to worry. I waited for twenty minutes and decided to walk back home by myself.

According to my father, he arrived at the doctor's office only five minutes after I had left. Unable to find me anywhere, he decided to go home. I had made up my mind to walk down the side streets since the national highway had too much traffic. The side streets had less traffic since it was snowing, and six inches of snow had already fallen on the ground.

After walking six miles, I lost my sense of direction since everything was covered in snow. I was cold, and I was lost. In the meantime, my parents reached out to a local radio station, which broadcast a missing child alert. Luckily, someone heard the broadcast and spotted me walking down the road in a distraught state. He picked me up and drove me to my parents' house, where many of our relatives had gathered and were waiting for me. As expected, my father grilled me about why I left and how I managed to return home. Nevertheless, everyone, including me, was relieved that I was home and safe.

Tragedy

The Shinano River, known as the Chikuma River in its upper reaches, is the longest and widest river in Japan. It is merely a quarter of a mile away from our family home. My brother and I played by the river often.

On March 16, 1964, I was eleven and my brother was thirteen. It was a rainy day, and my brother asked me if I wanted to go out and play by the river. At first I said no, but when I saw him walking toward the river with a neighborhood boy, I rushed to join them.

Earlier, we had dug a hole near the side of the river. It was a big, cavernous hole where the two of us could fit inside. That day, we were both playing inside the hole while the neighborhood friend was standing outside. He told us that he had to go to the bathroom, and I assumed that was what he was doing above us. For some reason, my brother started to poke away at the top of the hole with a stick. I urged him not to do it, but he did not listen to me. Suddenly, the top of the hole caved in. My brother and I were both trapped under the wet, heavy sand.

When we were playing in the hole on a previous day, my brother told me to place my arm in front of my mouth if the hole caved in. He said so in order for me to have space to breathe. When the top of the hole caved in that day, I immediately did what my brother had told me to do. I somehow managed to get free and told the neighborhood boy to run to the nearest house to get help.

When I looked back into the hole, I saw my brother's arm sticking out. I took his pulse, but he did not have one. I was in panic mode and do not know if I took his pulse correctly. I tried to dig him out, but the soil was so saturated with rainwater that I could do nothing.

In the meantime, rather than running to the nearest house to get help, the neighborhood boy ran home and stayed there. When he did not return with helpers, I ran to the nearest house and tried to get assistance. I guided them to the site where my brother was buried and ran straight back to our house to tell my parents what had happened at the river. As soon as my father heard me, he grabbed a rope and ran toward the river. I do not know why he grabbed the rope.

They managed to dig my brother out, but he was already dead. It must have been at least thirty minutes since the earth collapsed on my brother and me. My father carried him back to the house on his back. My brother's last words to me had been, "Help me."

Changing Expectations

My brother's death deeply impacted all of us. My mother was so grief-stricken that she isolated herself at home and concentrated on her work. She continued to grieve this way for three years.

It was an emotionally difficult time for me as well. Before my brother died, my parents always told me that I could do anything I wanted to do after finishing school. In Japan, tradition dictated that the eldest son would inherit the family's home and business, and he would take care of his elderly parents. With my brother gone, my parents' expectations placed a great deal of pressure on me. I tried to spend the least amount of time with them and often isolated myself in my room after dinner. I also got into the habit of locking the door to my bedroom whenever I left the house.

Junior High School Years (Grades Seven to Nine)

When I transitioned to junior high, I found myself attending six classes during the week and four classes on Saturdays. As in elementary school, lunch was served free of charge.

As an elementary school student, my dream was to become a professional baseball player. Baseball was a major extracurricular activity for me back then. I was the catcher for my team.

In junior high school, however, I joined the boys' basketball team. Normally, classes finished by 3:30 in the afternoon. From 4 p.m. to 6:30 p.m., we practiced hard, six days a week including Saturdays. By the time I got home, it was already past 7 p.m. But I could not get along with one of the senior team members, so I quit the team halfway through eighth grade.

Corporal Punishment in School

In Japan, English is a mandatory class for both junior high school and high school students. When I started the seventh grade, I was very excited about learning English and excelled in it. This was when my crazy side began to manifest.

Our science teacher believed in corporal punishment, and he had no qualms about dishing it out. Anyone who misbehaved in class became his victim. A person like this would certainly be disqualified as a teacher today, but this happened a long time ago.

The physical abuse he unleashed on us included pinching our cheeks, arms, and other body parts; kicking our legs; hitting our skulls with a clenched fist and his middle knuckle pointing out; and punching our temples with both fists. I was always on the top of his target list.

One day, he caught me doing something he did not like. He started walking toward me with his fists clenched, and I knew exactly what he planned to do. He came up behind me and tried to strike my temples. Without looking back, I felt his fists moving toward my head and perfectly timed moving my head forward to avoid getting hit. Pow! His fists collided with each other really hard, and it was easy to tell that he was in a lot of pain. Mission accomplished!

He walked away after kicking my leg as hard as he could. My fellow students were stunned and speechless. I talked to my homeroom teacher about the science teacher's violent nature, but he did not do anything about it. After this incident, I never bothered to look at the science teacher or the blackboard while in class. I did not even take notes. I just sat there being quiet. It was my way of giving him the silent treatment. Despite this, he still gave me a B! When graduation day came, I approached him, screamed obscenities in his face, and showered him with lewd gestures.

Preparing for the High School Entrance Examination

Even though upper-secondary education (high school) was not compulsory in Japan, there was intense competition to get into popular high schools, and students who wished to enroll were required to take an entrance examination. In my last year of junior high school, I had to prepare for the high school entrance examination. I studied past midnight every day. Until that point, I had 20/20 vision, but the intense studying damaged my eyesight. I have to wear glasses, which began in my first year in high school.

When I first began junior high school, I was an average student overall. By the time graduation came around, in a class of 300 students, I was in the top 10. My homeroom teacher assured my father that I would be accepted to the best public high school in Nagano Prefecture, Nagano High School. But I was concerned about whether or not I could attain a score high enough to be admitted to that school, so I selected another elite high school, Yashiro Senior High School. Back in those days, students could apply to multiple private high schools, but they were permitted to apply to only one public high school each year. Unfortunately, the educational level of the private schools in Nagano Prefecture was not that high at that time. If I had applied and not gotten into Nagano High School,

I would have had to wait one more year to try again. I simply did not want to take that risk.

High School Years (Grades Ten through Twelve)

The Japanese school year begins on April 1. Eager parents purchase new school uniforms, clothes, watches, fountain pens, and shoes for their children in anticipation of the new school year. On a warm spring day, with the cherry blossoms in full bloom, we attended the school entrance ceremony along with some other parents. The ceremony was usually held in the school gymnasium.

Attending a new school gave me a fresh start. My high school was located nearly four miles from my parents' house. I pedaled to school and back on my new bicycle, regardless of the weather. I rode on the two-lane national highway most of the way to school. Even though it was a national highway, it was not very wide, and the bicycle lane was barely three feet wide. It was very dangerous, particularly when the weather turned inclement. One of my friends was hit from behind by a car as he was riding his bicycle. On rainy days, I had to ride my bike while holding an umbrella in one hand. I hated the wind, because I was always riding to and from school against the wind.

Social Window Snafu

In my sophomore year, I had my eye on a cute high school girl who always waited at a bus stop beside the national highway. On a bright and sunny day, I was in a good mood while pedaling down the national highway. As usual, the girl was standing at the bus stop. I noticed that she was glancing at me more than usual. As I continued riding, about a quarter of a mile away, I felt an unusual breeze in between my legs. When I looked down, I realized that my zipper (commonly called a social window in Japanese) was open wide, like the mouth of a crocodile! I was devastated, because my opportunity to make a potential love connection was dashed. From that day forward, I changed my commuting time to avoid her.

Freshman Initiation

Each year at Yashiro Senior High School, in April, the freshmen assembled in the baseball field for initiation by the senior members of the *oendan* (cheering squad). Unlike an American cheerleading squad, their Japanese counterparts rely on making a lot of noise with taiko drums, blowing horns, waving flags and banners, and yelling through plastic megaphones. We were required to attend our school baseball team's away games and cheer for our players along with the oendan.

Everyone was afraid of the oendan as they had a reputation for intimidating students like a gang of thugs. During initiation, I managed to capture the attention of one of the squad members because I was not cheering enthusiastically enough. He walked over to me and screamed in my ear, "You are not cheering loud enough. Can you do it [expletive]?" It was obvious he was trying to intimidate me, but his tactic did not work. I responded rather rudely in an equally loud voice, "Yeah!" My response agitated him so much that he looked as if he was going to hit me. My fellow freshmen who witnessed this confrontation were shocked and expected to see me get hit. Fortunately, he changed his mind and walked away. I believe he might have been intimidated by my nonchalant attitude.

Good Judoka

A judo practitioner is known as a *judoka* in Japan. Judo exploded in the U.S. and across the globe during the 1950s and '60s. Judo became an Olympic sport and debuted in 1964 at the Tokyo Summer Olympic Games.

In my high school, we were required to take judo lessons twice a week for three months during the winter. Although I was just 5'7" tall and weighed 130 pounds, I was good at judo. During our class tournament I defeated five opponents, one after the other.

What on Earth Is a Seesaw?

As I wrote earlier, Yashiro Senior High School was one of the elite high schools in Nagano Prefecture. Most graduates went on to attend reputable colleges. After entering the school, I learned that I ranked 265th among the 315 freshmen admitted to Yashiro that year based on their entrance examination scores. Even though English was my favorite subject, I did not do well on the English test as there was a word in the reading comprehension section that I had never encountered before. I wondered, "What on earth is a seesaw?"

Later, after knowing where I placed, I felt a shiver run down my spine. Had I applied to Nagano High School, which admitted 410 freshman students, I probably would not have made it. I felt lucky that I did not choose that school and opted for Yashiro instead.

Like junior high schools, the public high schools in Japan taught a mandatory curriculum. The curriculum included nine subjects: Japanese,

English, mathematics, geology, history (Japanese and world), physics, chemistry, physical education, and art. The class schedules were basically identical to those in junior high.

The college entrance examination covered Japanese, English, mathematics, and history. History could be replaced by chemistry or physics depending on your major.

My high school life was mostly uneventful.

Extra-Curricular Activities

Shogi Kishi (Shogi Player)

Shogi, also known as Japanese chess, is the most popular chess variant native to Japan, and it has been around in its current form since the sixteenth century. I began playing shogi when I was thirteen and continued to play extensively until I was sixteen years old, aspiring to become a *puro kishi* (professional shogi player).

The things that differentiate shogi from regular chess are:

> 1. Shogi utilizes more pieces, and different numbers of familiar pieces: the *fu* (pawn, 9); *kyosha* (lance, 2); *keima* (knight, 2); *gin* (silver general, 2); *kin* (gold general, 2); *kaku* (bishop, 1); *hisha* (rook, 1); and *gyoku* (king, 1). The movements of some pieces in shogi are different than the movements of the corresponding pieces in chess.

> 2. Draws are not offered in shogi. Usually, the match is decided in over one hundred moves.

3. In shogi, you can use your opponent's captured pieces, which makes the game more complicated than regular chess.

4. Professional shogi players are well-paid, but attaining professional status requires years of training. Professionals are ranked between the fourth and ninth degrees, and their rankings differ from those of amateurs. Unless you attain the fourth degree by age twenty-five, you will automatically be expelled from the league.

Players ranked from the first to the third degrees are not considered professionals, and they do not earn any money. A fourth-degree professional player can easily beat a top-ranked amateur player. These days, kids often start playing shogi when they are just four or five years old.

When I was fifteen years old, I attended the monthly Nagano Regional Shogi Tournament held in Nagano City. It was a 15-minute train ride from my parents' house. I was practically the youngest player among those who participated in the tournament. The $2 participation fee included lunch.

If a player made it to the finals, he played eight matches in about six hours, which was physically and emotionally grueling. I always played well during the tournaments.

Once, I advanced to the final and had to compete against an adult player from Tokyo. During the match we were surrounded by ten or more adult onlookers. Unfortunately, I lost after a terribly challenging match. The biggest disappointment was that the winner was awarded a nice big plaque, and the runner-up (me) received a flimsy t-shirt. I played hard during this match and was awarded only a flimsy t-shirt. Until I started playing shogi extensively, I never realized that mentally challenging games like shogi consumed so much energy.

When I was sixteen years old, I participated in the first National High School Japanese Shogi Tournament held at Showa Yakukka Pharmaceutical College in Tokyo. I attended the two-day event with other high school students from Nagano. Although I enjoyed the experience immensely, I lost the first match. After returning home, I gave up the idea of becoming a professional player. I finally realized that there were way too many young, talented shogi players out there. I decided to continue to play shogi, but only as a hobby. I still play the game online.

Chess Challenge, 1970

During the summer of 1970, I had an opportunity to spend a week with an American family in Orange County, California. There, I met a 16-year-old high school student named Bruce. He was eager to teach me how to play regular chess. He used the first game to teach me the movements of the various chess pieces and the strategies involved. It was not surprising that I lost the first game.

I managed to beat him during the second game, and I continued winning thereafter. Bruce lost ten consecutive games to me, but he kept challenging me. He was clearly embarrassed to lose to a beginner.

Chess Challenge, 1975

In 1975, I stayed at an American friend's father's house for a few months while attending California Polytechnic State University (Cal Poly) in San

Luis Obispo (SLO), California. He was an avid chess player and wanted to play with me. Since I had not played regular chess since 1970, I had to relearn how to play the game.

After a few games, I got my mojo back and started winning. Naturally, this displeased him. We played every day for a week, and I was convinced that I would never lose to him. I boldly declared that if we played ten games consecutively, I would easily beat him without sustaining any losses. He took up the challenge. After I won six games in a row, he became frustrated and attempted to cheat during the seventh game. His dishonesty really upset me. I was rather temperamental at that age, and I reacted by flipping the chess board over, sending the chess pieces flying all over the place. I garnished that with a series of expletives and topped it off by giving him the middle finger. Naturally, he ordered me to move out the next day.

Misadventures with My Motorcycle

I entered a phase of being obsessed with motorcycles. At the age of sixteen, after I incessantly pestered my parents, they purchased a small Suzuki 70cc motorcycle for me.

Before I received my first motorcycle and earned my motorcycle driver's license, I practiced riding my father's motorcycle in my mother's orchard. One evening, while I was out riding, I mishandled the bike and ended up in the small stream running alongside the orchard.

My mother witnessed the accident and immediately rushed into the house to alert my father, who happened to be taking a bath at that time. What happened next shocked me more than the accident itself. I saw my father running toward me completely naked. Luckily, I was not injured.

Once I received my first motorcycle, I modified it to my liking. I painted the gas tank gold, changed the handlebar to a flat version, and installed a red seat cover. I also made the muffler louder, which later got me in trouble with the police for having an excessively noisy motorcycle.

A friend and I often toured various places together on my bike. One day, as we were returning home after a typical excursion, I accidentally drove into the rear bumper of the car in front of me. I tended to get distracted when I had a passenger with me. Fortunately, neither one of us was injured. I just bent the front forks of my motorcycle.

During my senior year in high school, I commuted to and from school on my motorcycle, but I did not have a school permit to do so. One winter afternoon, as I was returning home from school, a small truck seemed to appear out of nowhere. I could not avoid crashing into its front fender. The impact knocked me off of my bike, and my body slid on the road for six to eight feet. Fortunately, I was not riding very fast as I did not have a helmet on.

The uncontrolled skid tore the left leg of my school uniform pants and caused the skin on my upper thigh to scrape off. After obtaining the driver's name and phone number, I had to leave the scene as soon as possible so no one would report me to the school. After I arrived home, I immediately rushed up to my room so my parents would not see me. I did not want them to worry. (However, I did tell them about the accident later on. I negotiated with the driver and received $20 for a new pair of pants.)

In my room, I assessed the injury to my leg. I was in a lot of pain. I bandaged my leg as best I could and thought about what to do with my torn uniform pants. I did not have a spare pair. I pulled out my old uniform pants, which happened to be the same size as the torn pair. The left pant leg was still in good shape and provided the replacement material I needed for my torn pair. I carefully undid the stitches from top to bottom on the left sides of both the old and damaged pairs. I aligned the replacement material with the torn side of the pants and set about sewing it on my mother's manual foot pedal sewing machine. Fortunately for me, she stored it in my room. At this point, I was happy that I had received a B in sewing class when I was a sixth grader. I managed to perfectly repair my torn pair of pants.

To this day, I still have a big scar on my leg from that accident. When people see the scar and ask me how I got it, I tell them that I was shot with a big handgun. I am such a fibber sometimes!

Second Motorcycle

One day, as I was riding my motorcycle through our neighborhood, I found an abandoned motorcycle. It was already modified and perfect for motocross. I did not have any money, but when I got home, I found a 1964 Tokyo Olympics silver coin in a drawer in the living room. My father had paid $10 for it.

I took the coin without my parents' knowledge and struck a deal with the motorcycle's owner. He agreed to trade the motorcycle for the silver coin. My parents did not know where I got the motorcycle, and they never asked how I paid for it. When I get an idea, I have to accomplish it right away.

One night, after my parents had gone to bed, I felt an urge to modify my newly acquired motorcycle. I snuck out my second-floor bedroom window, walked across the roof, and climbed down the persimmon tree to get to the ground. My motorcycle was parked between the buildings. It had a two-stroke engine, and I was determined to increase its performance. I cut the piston skirt to increase the engine's gasoline/air mixture intake, which resulted in increased performance. Once the job was done, I followed the same path back to my room.

My friends and I rode this motorcycle a lot on the Chikuma riverbed, jumping over five-foot-high vegetation. Several times in the middle of night, I had urges to ride the motorcycle. It was not street legal since it did not have a headlight, a brake light, or blinkers. As before, I quietly climbed out of the window with my portable radio in hand and down to the ground to reach my motorcycle. I tied the radio to the handlebar and pushed the bike to the riverbank a quarter of a mile away from my parents' house.

It was midnight, and the river bank was a scary place to be as there was no one around. I turned on my radio and rode my bike for about two miles, reaching speeds of 15 miles per hour, until I reached the area under the big bridge. I spent about 15 minutes there and came back home. I simply wanted to do this to prove to myself that I was not afraid of the dark. However, it was pretty scary since the top of the river bank was narrow, unpaved, and some sections were covered with six-foot high brush.

Pigeon Fancier

During my freshman year in high school, I kept up to ten pigeons as a hobby. I constructed a nice pigeon house under one of my mother's apple trees using salvaged wood I found around my parents' house. The structure measured four feet high, four feet wide, and four feet deep. It sat about three feet above the ground. At first, I was very devoted to my hobby and raised a few squabs or baby pigeons. There were occasions when I raced them.

However, as growing boys often do, I eventually lost interest in the hobby. One at a time, the pigeons left, except for one. My father eventually got fed up with me. One day, after I returned home from school on my bicycle, I noticed a pile of bird feathers on the ground of my mother's apple orchard. It struck me as strange. As soon as I walked into the house, my father called out to me, telling me that he had "prepped it." I asked him what he meant. He told me to go into the kitchen and take a look.

When I walked into the kitchen, I saw a plucked little bird nicely placed on a plate with its legs up in the air like a Thanksgiving turkey. I knew immediately that it was my pet pigeon. I was furious. Why had my father done this? But as the saying goes, "It's no use crying over spilled milk." I cooked the plucked pigeon and ate it. Perhaps my craziness is something I inherited from my father.

The Dutch Wife

When I was seventeen years old, I visited an adult toy store in Nagano City with two of my close friends. When we arrived, we noticed that the store was divided into two sections, the papa section and the mama section. Naturally, we gravitated toward the papa section in search of a Dutch wife (an archaic Japanese term for a blow-up sex doll). We found the store clerk and repeatedly asked him whether or not the doll came with "it." He never lost his imperturbable demeanor and met our youthful exuberance with the same answer each time, "You will find out after you purchase it."

Uncertain of what to do next, we went outside to discuss whether or not we should purchase the Dutch wife. The decision was unanimous, and we decided to take the plunge. We handed $40 dollars to the clerk, which was a considerable sum of money in those days, and hoped that our luck would not betray us.

As soon as she was ours, we rushed outside and quickly went about the business of determining whether or not she was equipped with "it." Our hearts sank in deep disappointment when we discovered that our new friend was not so equipped. The doll with the beautiful Caucasian face and blonde hair eventually became mine after I purchased it from my friends.

Like a Rolling Stone, or a Head Full of Rocks

During my sophomore year in high school, I purchased a Mazda 360 coupe for $50 from a friend. It was a two-seater kei car (short for *keijidosha*), the smallest highway-legal passenger car, and had restricted dimensions and engine capacity.

Even though the car had a license plate attached, its *shaken* (vehicle registration) had expired. In Japan, when a car is first registered, the shaken/registration is good for three years. After that, the vehicle registration must be renewed every two years for the life of the car. The Mazda had been sitting in my friend's yard for at least five years, and it was not drivable when I purchased it. I gathered my friends together and asked them to push the car half a mile to my parents' house while I steered.

From that point on I visited the junkyard on a regular basis, scavenging for parts to repair the Mazda's engine. I managed to fix everything but the starter. When I was alone, I had to use a crank bar to start the engine. If I had someone with me, we pushed to start the vehicle.

iv. A light blue Mazda 360 Coupe, similar to my car, auto show in Los Angeles

Although I had a motorcycle license, I was still too young to get a driver's license. I did not let that little detail stop me from driving my car around the back roads. One day, I played hooky from school and went for a drive with my friend, who played hooky from work. We were enjoying driving along the top of the river bank when I momentarily stopped paying attention to my driving. By the time I realized what was happening, the car was skidding sideways. Within seconds, the world outside my vehicle was revolving. The car rotated two and a half times before it finally landed upside down on the gravel road below.

I immediately rushed out of the car through the open door and waited for my friend to come out. Ten seconds later, he emerged from the car and hopped around in pain. Despite this, he did not appear to be seriously injured.

Several farmers came to see what had happened, and I begged them to help me right my car. We managed to flip the Mazda upright, but I soon realized that the roof was smashed in. Amazingly, despite everything, the windshield had not broken.

I managed to squeeze back into the driver's seat, and my friend and I sped away before the police could get there. That would have been a major headache as the car was not registered, and I did not have a driver's license.

We drove to the other side of the riverbank. I parked the car as close to the edge of the road as possible since dump trucks often used that street. My friend and I walked to our respective houses; no one other than us and the farmers knew about the accident. As I had done earlier with my motorcycle mishaps, I never told my parents about this accident.

That night I suffered from a severe headache, caused by hitting my head hard against the roof of the car as it rolled. I was unable to turn my head to either side and tears welled up in my eyes. I was in such excruciating pain that I thought I was going to die.

The next morning, I felt a little better and decided to go to school. That afternoon I was miserable, still unable to turn my head, and the headache was pounding in my head as before. I was also determined not to say a word to my parents about what had happened.

Four days later, I felt much better and I decided to go and see my car. I returned to the site where I had left the car. As I looked around for my Mazda, I heard the noise of wiper blades moving. When I looked down the slope of the riverbank, I saw my car on its side at the bottom. It had slid fifteen feet, and the wiper blades were swinging back and forth on the windshield. I shut off the wiper blades and left the scene.

The following day, I asked six classmates to help me pull my car up out off the bottom of the riverbank. After school, the seven of us went to the site on our bikes. It was evident that we would not be able to pull the car up without a sturdy rope. I rushed home to get a rope, and while I was searching for one, my father found me and asked me what I was doing. I had no choice but to tell him what had transpired.

However, I slightly altered the story and said that I had parked my car on the top of the river bank and someone pushed it down the embankment. My father grabbed a long, sturdy rope and we got into his truck. When we arrived at the site, my classmates were still there. Using his truck and the rope, my father, my classmates, and I managed to pull the car up to the top of the river bank in fifteen minutes. I thanked my classmates for their help, and my father towed my car home with me sitting in the driver's seat.

My First Chop Top

I loved my little car so much that I did not have the heart to junk it. Instead, I decided to chop the crushed top off with a chisel. I drove the car topless for some time, but it did not feel safe with the body flexing back and forth like a boat rolling in rough seas.

I thought I would remedy the problem by affixing the doors to the body of the car with heavy wire. This minimized the flexing issue, but then there was the matter of driving around in rainy weather.

I solved this problem by securing a wooden door with six glass panels over the driver's and passenger's seats. It was very odd looking, but I was able to drive my car for a few more months. I eventually grew tired of it and junked it for $10.

Saitama

College Years

International College of Commerce and Economics
(April 1970 - February 1972)

As I wrote earlier, I studied very hard to prepare for my high school entrance examination, only to have my vision deteriorate to the point where I needed to wear glasses. Initially, my objective was to get accepted into *Jochi Daigaku* (Sophia University) and major in a foreign language, English. At that time, Jochi Daigaku was the best school in Japan for foreign language studies. To meet this objective, I studied very hard as soon as my senior year in high school commenced. However, I later decided that I did not want to force myself through the rigors of studying for yet another entrance examination. Instead, I found a new private college in Saitama, just 20 miles north of central Tokyo.

International College of Commerce and Economics (currently known as Tokyo International University) was only four years old. All applicants were required to submit a letter of recommendation from their high school. They also had to take an English language test and a Japanese essay test to be admitted. I was exempted from taking the English language test as I had already obtained my English proficiency test certificate. The only thing that remained was the Japanese essay test.

As I waited for my turn to take the essay test, there were concerned and anxious parents in the room with me. Some were curious about why I was there, and they kept glancing over at me.

I easily passed the exam and was accepted into the college. The tuition was relatively expensive, but my parents were willing to pay it.

v. My boarding house in Saitama

Life in a Private Boarding House

I was fortunate that two friends from my high school also chose to attend International College of Commerce and Economics. The school was approximately 100 miles from my parents' house in Nagano, and it had an enrollment of about 1,200 students.

In mid-March, my friends and I traveled to Kawagoe City in Saitama Prefecture and looked for a place to live while we attended college. We found a two-story, privately-owned boarding house right outside the college's back gate. The house had nine rooms, each measuring six tatami mats. The Japanese refer to the size of a room by the number of tatami mats that fit inside it. Each tatami mat measures three feet by six feet. There were water faucets and sinks in the hallways on both floors. There was a toilet at the end of each hallway. The house did not have a shower, but there was a typical, small Japanese bathtub. To keep the hot water in the tub clean for multiple people, we were required to clean our bodies first before jumping into the tub. Sometimes, I took a bath with my housemates. The house was owned and run by a 32-year-old divorcee who had a five-year-old son.

One day toward the end of March, my father and I packed his truck with my belongings (desk, chair, bedding, stereo, clothes, and various small items) and drove almost four hours to the boarding house. My father helped unload my things and we placed them in my room. When we were done, he returned home. I had arrived first, followed by my two friends from Nagano. Nine of us lived in the boarding house, seven freshmen and two sophomores who had stayed on from the previous year.

Each room had a closet measuring one tatami mat where we kept our bedding. There was no bed, so we slept on the floor on traditional Japanese bedding. Each morning when I woke up, I had to fold my bedding and place it in the small closet. Some days I was too lazy to do it and just left it on the floor.

Room and board cost $165 a month. We were provided with breakfast and dinner in the dine-in kitchen every day except Sundays. The lady owner was a pretty good cook. For lunch, I went up to my room and enjoyed a few slices of toast with a cup of coffee. That was the typical lunch for college students in those days.

My Housemates

My housemates hailed from different parts of Japan and had different backgrounds. We had a collection of students from Nagano, Shizuoka, Niigata, Nagasaki, and Ishikawa. We seldom talked to the two sophomore residents due to the difference in our ages.

I discovered some interesting things about my housemates who were high school friends from Nagano. The first one cried whenever he got drunk. His room was next to mine, and we got along well together. I learned years later that he was gay and had never married.

My second friend was a year older than I, and he was like my brother. He had a rather unique talent of being able to fall asleep while lying on the floor sideways and holding his head up with one arm. He was able to sleep in that position for hours. He was funny, too.

During our sophomore year, he came to visit me at my parents' house during the summer break. His parents lived only fifteen miles from my home. In the middle of the night, we set out on my motorcycle and went to the nearby riverbank. We were on a quest to find a couple romantically engaged in their car late at night. We spotted a car parked a quarter of a mile away. I turned off the headlight and stopped my bike about 100 yards behind the vehicle. My friend and I got off the motorcycle and crawled on our stomachs in what is known as the "army crawl" until we reached the car. Before we reached our target, however, my friend slipped down the slope once.

When we were outside the parked vehicle, we quietly and carefully placed our ears on the side of the car door to see if we could listen in on what was transpiring inside. To our disappointment, they were just talking to each other.

We returned home and decided to take a bath together before going to sleep. As soon as we undressed, we both burst into hysterical laughter. Both of our behinds were covered in huge bumps. The Nagano mosquitos by the riverbank had found our derrieres irresistible as we crawled on our bellies.

Back in our boarding house, I inflated the Dutch wife I had purchased in my younger days and placed her prominently in the corner of my room. One day, the same friend asked me if he could borrow it. I agreed, and he took the doll into an empty room next to mine. While it was in his possession, I heard all sorts of squeaking noises coming from that room, similar to the sounds you hear when you rub a balloon. In about 15 minutes, my friend returned to my room with a big grin on his face. He looked happy but a little exhausted.

Sadly, he passed away from leukemia one year after I quit college. It felt like I had lost another brother.

Another housemate came all the way from Nagasaki, 598 miles from Saitama. He was a soft-spoken person. We did not have a lot in common and did not spend too much time together.

Another housemate hailed from Niigata, just on the other side of the border of Nagano. He was friendly, so we got along well and did a lot of things together. One day, I needed an athletic supporter for my physical education class and he let me borrow his. Unfortunately, it was unwashed and had a smudge of fecal matter on it. I did not care and wore it anyway.

The housemate from Ishikawa was one year older than the other freshman boarders. As a high school student, he had the opportunity to travel to the United States as an exchange student on a scholarship. This guy was addicted to working out and he often flexed his muscles.

Our housemate from Shizuoka was into the latest fashions and tried to act cool all the time. He had some behaviors that were uniquely his own, including walking around his room while pleasuring himself.

The Sophomore

Our boarding house catered primarily to freshmen. The year before we moved in, there were nine other freshmen living at the boarding house. Seven of the freshmen moved out, but two remained at the house through their sophomore year.

One of the former boarders was known by his nickname, Chin. Chin in Japanese means rare, unique, or strange. He was given this nickname by his housemates because, frankly, he was the epitome of what the name implied. He visited our boarding house occasionally, and when he did, we addressed him as Chin-san, because he was one year older than we were.

Chin-san was the only child of a wealthy family in Nagasaki. His mother had practically done everything for him until he moved into the boarding house. Chin-san was incapable of doing most things for himself as his mother had fed, dressed, bathed, and handled most of life's necessities for him. In fact, Chin-san did not even know how to tie his shoelaces. During mealtime at the boarding house, he dropped food continuously. He did not know how to properly handle a pair of chopsticks.

When Chin-san first arrived at the boarding house, he did not understand the difference between a men's urinal and a toilet. A story circulated claiming that he defecated in the men's urinal.

Another story that was going around the boarding house alleged that he visited a bordello and was refused service due to the size of his member. Apparently, the prostitute was afraid that he would injure her.

One day, I visited Chin-san at his apartment. I knocked on the door several times, but he refused to answer. I knew that he was home so I continued knocking on the door. He finally opened the door after ten minutes or so with an exhausted look on his face. Seeing him this way, I immediately knew what he had been up to.

While inside his apartment, I happened to pull open a desk drawer. Inside were two stacks of tissues. One stack was comprised of coarse gray tissue papers while the other stack contained soft white tissue papers. Puzzled, I asked him why he kept two stacks of different tissues in his desk drawer. Initially, he refused to answer, but my persistence pried an answer out of him. He said that he used the tissues to clean up after pleasuring himself. The soft white tissues were reserved for the times when he fantasized about a beautiful lady and the coarse gray tissues were used when he imagined an unattractive woman.

The Shogi Bet

Chin-san was an avid shogi player and we played a few games together. Once I determined his skill level, I challenged him to a game where we wagered our hair. Whoever lost would shave off his hair. He agreed, and we began the game.

We were in my room at the boarding house and there was one bystander with us. After forty moves, it became obvious that he was going to lose the game. He grew restless and offered me $10 to call off the bet. Naturally, I refused. Then he upped the ante and said he would shave off his pubic hair and give me $10. I declined that offer as well. Afterward, he insisted that he needed to go to the bathroom, so I let him. After a minute had passed, he did not return. I became suspicious and asked the bystander to come with me while we investigated Chin-san's whereabouts.

Chin-san saw us approaching and rushed into a nearby room. We pursued him. He opened a window and tried to escape. Half of his body was out of the window when we grabbed him by the legs so he would not fall. We were on the second floor, and it was a nine-foot drop to the ground.

He pleaded with us to let him go, but we refused, fearing that he would fall and injure himself. We finally managed to pull him back inside and resumed the game. As projected, Chin-san lost.

Two days later, he shaved his head. In Japan, one of the most earnest, old-school ways to apologize is by shaving your head. Obviously, this isn't something people do for honest mistakes or minor screw-ups, but when they want to go all-out in saying they are sorry. To Chin-san, there could be nothing worse than losing a bet to a freshman and having to shave his head.

Good Times With My Housemates

With the exception of the freshman from Nagasaki, who was unathletic, the rest of us played baseball and soccer. We ran outdoors starting at about

8:00 p.m. and covered two miles. We were very competitive and always ran at full speed.

Some of us played mahjong occasionally. We enjoyed our friendships and each other's company.

Lost in Tokyo

I decided to go to Tokyo one day and visit a friend. I left the boarding house at 9 a.m. and reached Tokyo in 40 minutes by public train. I exited the train at the Ikebukuro train station and got lost.

A crowd surged past me, and I got swallowed up in the swarm. I assumed that if I followed the crowd, they would lead me to the exit gate. Well, this innocent boy from Nagano couldn't have been more mistaken. As people turned off and went up and down various stairs, the massive swarm gradually grew thinner. I continued to follow the smaller crowd for about 200 feet until we reached an exit gate. I was the last person in the crowd to proceed through the exit gate. However, when I gave my train ticket to the ticketing agent before walking through the gate, he grabbed me by the arm and asked, "Where did you come from?"

I was totally discombobulated and had no clue where I was, so I pointed my finger toward the direction from which I came. The agent asked me again, "Where did you come from?" This time, I responded, "That way!" He then proceeded to tell me that I was holding a ticket for a public train and I was at the gate for a private train station.

I apologized by bowing deeply. I explained to him that I was just a country boy from Nagano, and I had simply followed the crowd to get here. The agent did not want to devote any more time to a country boy like me, so he let me go. It was a totally humiliating experience.

At College

In the early 1970s, student demonstrations were common on college campuses. The wave of demonstrations finally reached our college, but I was not interested in politics and did not pay any attention to it.

Classes began at 9 a.m., and since the boarding house was so close to the college, I got up at 8:40 a.m., got ready, and ran to my first class. I was thoroughly enjoying my time at the boarding house with my mates; therefore, studying was not my first priority.

Large classrooms could accommodate up to 300 students, and representatives from the administration office took attendance. They distributed attendance cards to the students; we wrote our names and signed the cards. To prevent students from skipping classes, different colored cards were used each day. However, some students managed to accumulate a collection of cards in various colors and submitted attendance cards on their friends' behalf. One student carried an attaché case in which cards of various colors were nicely arranged. I assumed that his parents owned a printing shop.

After the administration office representatives left, some students also departed, but I stayed in the back of the classroom to play shogi or read newspapers. I seldom read any of the textbooks in preparation for my classes, and I rarely took notes in class since most of the professors gave the same tests time after time. Just before the midterm and final tests were to be administered, we borrowed notes from students who had taken the tests earlier. So, I basically studied the night before the exams.

I took French 1 and 2, but the only phrase I remember is *je t'aime* (I love you). Still, I managed to maintain a B average during my two years in college. However, there was some dishonesty involved; I cheated twice. Both incidents involved the French examinations. Even though I dutifully attended every French lesson, I never paid attention to what was going on in class. Therefore, I did not learn anything and had to resort to cheating to pass the French midterm and final exams.

The examinations were administered in a huge classroom, and staff from the administration office constantly walked around ensuring that nobody was cheating. I had to come up with a means to beat that system.

I purchased an enormous 2"x3" eraser, to which I affixed my cheat sheet. Before affixing it, I wrote on it the information I needed for the test. To cram as much info as possible onto the limited space, I held the fine point fountain pen at a 180-degree angle to make the ink flow in an even finer line. When I placed the eraser on the desk with the cheat sheet side down, it looked like an ordinary, large eraser. After the administration staff member passed my desk, I placed the eraser under my palm and flipped it over to read what I had written. My plan proved to be a success, and I did not arouse any suspicions.

My Western History Professor

History had always been my least favorite subject in school, but I never failed to attend my Western history course as the instructor was so entertaining. He was in his early eighties and commuted to work from

Tokyo. He had a bald head with only a few strands of hair remaining and wore dark-rimmed glasses.

I hardly ever paid attention to his lectures, but I enjoyed his jokes. It seemed that he had encountered a beautiful lady on the train one day and could not forget her. He named her Mary, and he talked about her often during class. He was completely mesmerized by her.

Unlike my other classes, I did not do well on my Western history midterm. The instructor was old-fashioned. Instead of administering the same test year after year like the other professors, he distributed a sheet of paper with one sentence written at the top. He wanted us to write essays for both the midterm and final examinations.

The single sentence for the final examination read, "Discuss how Western civilization evolved and what impact it had on human existence." I was not prepared to discuss this topic, but I had to write something. I began my essay in this way. "I apologize because I do not know anything about Western civilization, but I will expound on the Roman Empire instead."

I practically filled the entire sheet of paper with all that I knew about the topic, and I used the remaining space at the bottom of the page to draw a caricature of the professor. The drawing featured the professor's bald head with three strands of hair sticking up. Both of his hands were up in the air and the speech bubble next to the drawing included the following words, "Mary, I love you!" Was this the ultimate act of sarcastic defiance? I took a gamble and it paid off. I received a B for the course.

Bournemouth, England

One day in January 1971, I saw a newspaper advertisement for Bournemouth, England, a coastal resort town located 94 miles southwest of London. It promoted a three-week stay in England to learn English, followed by stopovers in France and Italy for one week on the return trip to Japan. The cost of the trip was $3,000, a sizeable sum of money in the early 1970s.

I really wanted to go, so one evening I called my father in Nagano and explained the program to him in detail. He listened and afterwards asked me what the trip would cost. When I gave him the figure, he said he would send me the money right away without even talking to my mother about it. It was very typical of my father.

Wise Guys in Ginza

On February 27, 1971, my two college friends and all six of my freshman housemates came to send me off at Haneda International Airport. Basically, we were all country boys, and we had never been to an international airport before. We thought this would be a good opportunity to initiate everyone and spend some time together in Tokyo before my departure to England.

Before going to the airport we decided to visit Ginza, Tokyo's most famous upscale shopping, dining, and entertainment district. It features numerous department stores, boutiques, art galleries, restaurants, night clubs, and cafes. On weekend afternoons, Ginza's central Chuo-Dori Street is closed to automobile traffic, and it becomes a large pedestrian zone.

On that Saturday at 5 p.m., we were totally overwhelmed by the number of people strolling in the streets, almost shoulder to shoulder. My mischievous side suddenly emerged, and I decided to prank the people walking in the street.

Suddenly, my friends and I stopped in the middle of the busy street and looked up at the sky without saying a word. We did this for about a minute or so. One by one, curious about why we were looking up, other people started to direct their gazes upwards. Soon, practically everyone around us was looking up at the sky with quizzical looks on their faces. By the time it was all done, approximately two hundred people had gathered around us, looking up at the sky.

We slowly slipped away from the crowd and laughed hysterically all the way to Haneda Airport.

School Life in Bournemouth

In Bournemouth, my accommodation was in a boarding house. An elderly woman, who cared for her sick, bedridden husband, ran it. I was told that I would be sharing the house with other foreign students, but when I arrived, I was the only one there. The lady provided me with simple breakfasts and dinners for the duration of my three-week stay. I was only permitted to take a shower twice a week.

On the first day of school we were given an English proficiency test. Fortunately, or unfortunately, my test scores placed me at the top of the class. Our teacher was Scottish, and eighty percent of the time I could not understand what he was saying because of his thick brogue. He also had the penmanship of a doctor. Deciphering his illegible handwriting on the blackboard was a real challenge.

I only looked forward to lunch in the cafeteria, where a couple of cute girls worked. On weekends, the trip organizer took us to visit Oxford and Soho. These neighborhoods are located just south of downtown London.

In Soho, I was completely shocked by the fact that I had to pay to use the public bathroom. I was equally disturbed by the fact that the top panel of the bathroom door had been removed. People, perfect strangers, were able to see me while I was in the bathroom. To me, the bathroom is a sacred place where I take care of business in private. This was not the case in Soho. I felt violated and embarrassed.

I was also surprised to meet a senior from my college in the class. He called himself John. He visited me in my boarding house after we returned from England, and I asked him why he called himself John. He told me that many foreigners had difficulty pronouncing his Japanese name, so he adopted an English name to make it easier for them.

He asked me to give him my English dictionary and what the first letter of my name was. I answered, "M," and he quickly flipped the pages to the section with words beginning with that letter. Glancing at the pages, he said, "Here we go! I have found a good name for you. You will call yourself Mickey from now on." The name stuck, and I have been calling myself Mickey ever since. Many of my friends do not know my real first name.

Visiting France for the First Time

At the end of three weeks, our English lessons in Britain finally concluded. We boarded an immense ferry and crossed the English Channel to France. While in Paris, we visited the typical tourist hotspots. I saw the Eiffel Tower and the Arc de Triomphe. At the Louvre Museum, I saw the sculpture of Venus de Milo and an ancient Egyptian mummy. We remained in France for three days, and what surprised me the most was the small stature of the French people. As we strolled through the streets of Paris, I initially thought that there were a lot of tourists from Japan visiting France, but they were Parisians. They were noticeably smaller than the British.

Coming of Age in Paris?

I met two other Japanese students while traveling in France. One of them was the same age as me, nineteen. The other was a year older. I couldn't be absolutely sure, but I thought they were both virgins, like me. The three of us eagerly strolled the streets of Paris together in search of suitable escorts to help us become men.

As we walked the streets, we saw that they were lined with call girls offering their services. Soon, we were approached by three ladies of the night singing the words "chinko, manko, chinko, manko." In Japanese, *chinko* refers to the male genital and *manko* refers to the female genital. I assumed these women had serviced many Japanese clients and had picked up their limited Japanese from them. Like any other red-blooded Japanese boys would do in a similar situation, we felt drawn to these girls due to their "Japanese language skills."

We negotiated a payment of $25 each for their services and proceeded to a hotel, where we crammed into a tiny elevator that barely accommodated six people as we willingly marched toward our virgin sacrifice ritual. We finally reached a sparsely furnished room with only two single beds placed three feet apart from one another and a plain sink. After we paid our fees, we cleaned ourselves in the water flowing from the faucet of the austere-looking sink. We responsibly donned our prophylactics and got ready to tackle the task at hand.

While I was on the floor being serviced and getting rug burns in places where I never imagined having rug burns, I looked up at my two friends to see how they were getting along. The older friend was busy on one of the beds with his bare behind rhythmically rising and falling. The friend who was my age sat on the edge of the other bed looking very forlorn as his partner worked frantically to bring him to working order.

After I observed this bizarre scene for ten minutes, one of our escorts declared, "Time is up!" Unfortunately, as I had been busy scrutinizing the situation around me, I did not have time to finish my work. Our older friend's performance remained unfinished as well. I looked down at my escort and attempted to negotiate additional time for another $5, but I was flatly refused.

I was frustrated, but I felt really bad for my friend who did not even have the opportunity to experience the warmth of a woman. Disappointed, we returned to our hotel.

Never Leave a Job Unfinished

When we arrived back at our hotel, I was enraged by what had transpired earlier that evening. Not wanting to leave a job unfinished, I decided to go out on my own. My soldier was still dressed in his raincoat, ready to tackle whatever duty I tasked him with.

I started down the street where we met our escorts earlier, but for some reason I lost my sense of direction and got lost. I soon found myself in a very deserted section of Paris and was approached by another woman in the same business. She began to speak to me in French, but I felt very uneasy in that part of town, so I walked on.

Suddenly, I was overcome by the urge to relieve myself, and I found a suitable spot in between some parked cars. While I was busy relieving myself, I sensed someone approaching me from behind. When I turned my head to look, I saw two French police officers standing behind me. I was shocked at the sight of the officers, and my soldier abandoned me by shrinking and taking cover. I thought I was going to be arrested.

Naturally, I was unable to communicate with them as the only French word I knew after taking two French classes was *je t'aime*. I didn't think it would be wise to use that phrase with the police, particularly under these circumstances.

After examining my passport, they finally let me go. Afterward, I returned to my hotel as fast as I could, but I have no recollection of exactly how I got there. It was 2 a.m. when I finally got to bed. Before falling asleep, I vowed that I would finish the job in Italy.

Next Stop, Italy

We rode the Eurail train from Paris to Rome the next day. As we had done in Paris, we visited the common sightseeing spots such as the Trevi Fountain, the Colosseum, and the Pantheon in Piazza della Rotonda. I enjoyed visiting these places. I did not like the fact that everywhere we went, we were surrounded by children begging for money. Also, the young Italian men spent an inordinate amount of time and energy chasing after women.

The Italian Job

During our visit to Rome, the public transportation workers were on strike, so we had to take a taxi to get around. We recruited a new guy replacing the person who botched the job in Paris. Three of us hailed a taxi and headed straight to the red-light district.

When we arrived, our older friend from Paris kept saying, "I can smell the whores!" Sure enough, we glimpsed two young Italian girls dressed in tight black hot pants signaling us for their services. We beckoned them over. As they crossed the street to meet us, they recruited another girl to join them. We negotiated 100 lira each for their services and hired two taxis to take the six of us to a hotel.

As our taxis drove away, we noticed a car with three or four young Italian men chasing us and shouting something in Italian. After five minutes, we managed to lose them and reached our destination. The hotel manager insisted on keeping our passports, but we vehemently refused. Ultimately, we gave in and surrendered our passports after we realized that we could not get a room otherwise.

Unlike in Paris, we were placed in separate rooms adorned with nice, romantic décor. This was the first time I encountered a bidet. I initially thought it was something to wash my face in. The lights were dimmed and there was a nice bed, so I did not have to worry about rug burns this time. I gave my partner my Japanese sheath, but she kept it and dressed my eager soldier with an Italian-made raincoat instead. Finally, I completed the job. I became a man at last.

My two companions were successful as well, and we all returned to our hotel with glowing smiles on our faces. We returned to Japan on March 27, 1971.

Six Weeks in Berkeley, California

In the summer of 1971, I was invited by a couple in their fifties to live in their house in Berkeley while attending adult school to learn English. Their names were Richard and Carolyn. Richard was a prominent architect and Carolyn worked as a garden designer. She designed one of the gardens at San Francisco's Golden Gate Park.

Richard and Carolyn lived in a large, custom-built house on a hill overlooking Berkeley. Their two-story home had three grand pianos. After I arrived, I was given a medium-sized bedroom in the basement. Their lifestyle and customs were unknown to me.

For example, during dinner, they typically devoted at least one hour to eating and talking. I, on the other hand, was used to wolfing down my food as quickly as possible. Once I finished eating, they often asked me if I wanted seconds, but I could not say yes. I was under the impression that it was bad manners to eat so much as a house guest. As a result, I typically felt hungry. Occasionally, I sneaked out of the house late at night and bought something to eat at the nearby liquor store.

Richard and Carolyn had two sons, Kris and Dan, and two daughters, Beverly and Amelia.

Their youngest son, Dan, was a student at University of California, Berkeley, and he was hitchhiking across Japan with two of his friends from school. Before I left for Berkeley, Dan and his friends stayed at my parents' house for a few days. Dan was a tall, skinny young man with long blonde hair. He often wore a leather headband, and his style appealed to me. It was a bohemian, hippie look.

On weekends we visited Richard and Carolyn's vacation home in Mendocino County, about 120 miles from Berkeley. It was a vast property with a main house and a guest house. Once, I asked Richard how much land he owned, and he responded, "As far as your eye can see." His land was heavily wooded. We often went down a steep cliff to their private beach and had barbeques with their relatives. Richard's brother owned a lot of property right next door. This was my first taste of the wealthy American lifestyle.

vi. With friends in London (I'm in the middle)

vii. Carolyn and Richard

viii. On vacation in Mendocino County

Introduction to Mary Jane

On one occasion, Richard and Carolyn's daughter, Beverly, and her friend accompanied us to the Mendocino property. The young ladies were in their early twenties. When evening fell, they came to the main house and asked me if I wanted to join their pot party. I hesitated, but my curiosity eventually got the best of me.

They started a fire in the fireplace to set the mood, then they educated me in the proper technique of smoking a joint. After the three of us passed a few joints around, I began laughing uncontrollably. Admittedly, I enjoyed the lightheadedness smoking pot produced and the food cravings which followed. We nibbled on some snacks and went outside for a walk. I realized I was walking like an ape, moving my body from side to side. For the first time in my life, I became stoned, and enjoyed it.

For the duration of my stay with Richard and Carolyn, I joined Kris, Beverly, and their friends for the pot parties they held once in a while at Kris's house.

I became fascinated by the ritual that took place prior to smoking pot. First, they closed all the windows and shut all the curtains. Next, they put some psychedelic records on the stereo, lit a few candles, and carefully placed them in the center of the living room floor. They turned off the lights, and we seated ourselves in a circle around the candles. Then the smoking began.

It was an enjoyable experience, but it always came with the risk of being arrested. That was why we closed all the windows and drew all of the curtains.

The Turning Point

While attending adult school in California, I met a brother and sister from Japan. They were of Korean ancestry and had been victimized and discriminated against due to anti-Asian sentiments while they lived in Boston. Berkeley offered them a completely different environment, and they both enjoyed living in California.

The three of us went to a bowling alley almost every day. One day, they asked me what I wanted to do after I finished adult school. I told them that I had to return to Japan and finish college. They insisted that I remain in the U.S. and go to college here. I explained to them that the situation was rather complicated. After my older brother passed away, I was the only child. It was my responsibility to take care of my aging parents. Also, there was the matter of paying for my education and living expenses. After listening to my concerns, they suggested I return to the U.S. and attend college. I had not even considered that possibility until they brought it up. In all likelihood, I probably would not be living here today if they had not advocated my return. Meeting them was a big turning point in my life.

On my way back from school, I strolled around the UC Berkeley campus, watched the demonstrators, and listened to people making speeches against the government. Nearby was the iconic Telegraph Avenue. The Telegraph Avenue district is revered as the place where the counterculture came to Berkeley, and it became a national phenomenon from there.

Teenagers and hippies congregated, sidewalks featured arts and crafts displays, and the smells of pot and incense wafted through the air. Long hair, bell bottom jeans, and psychedelic clothes were all new to this country boy from Japan. I truly enjoyed immersing myself in these surroundings. I never got into the politics of the time, but I embraced nonconformity as much as anyone else walking down those streets. To me, encountering the counter-culture lifestyle was a match made in heaven. I really enjoyed my time in Berkeley.

When I returned to Japan, I began mimicking the hippie lifestyle I had observed in Berkeley.

A Week in Anaheim, California

From Berkeley, I hopped on a Greyhound bus to Anaheim. I was met at the Greyhound station by the father of one of Dan's hitchhiking buddies in Japan. He was in his forties and balding. He came to pick me up in a convertible, and we drove to his residence in Anaheim Hills in style.

Anaheim Hills was an affluent area in Southern California, and every house had a swimming pool. Like the other homes in the area, his residence was situated on a hill overlooking the city of Anaheim. Standing in their beautiful kitchen, we saw the fireworks display at Disneyland from the window. The couple's son, Bruce, was the one I repeatedly beat at chess.

The family showed me around the city of Anaheim and fed me well. I purchased a leather headband and the Doors' single record, "Riders on the Storm," to bring back to Japan. I was very lucky to spend those early days in the U.S. with wealthy families. I vowed that I would return to the U.S. to attend college and someday live a life that matched the ones I had observed.

Back to School

When school started in the fall, my American influences were already detectable. I started wearing the leather headband I had purchased in Anaheim, California as my hair was already semi-long. I went to school wearing a pair of beach sandals or walking barefoot.

On the first day of English class, my professor quipped that there was a new girl in class. Actually, there were no female students. Everyone in the class turned around, looked at me, and laughed. I wasn't bothered by it at all because it made me happy to be recognized as a hippie.

Addicted to Pachinko

In addition to paying my tuition, my parents also sent me $300 a month for living expenses. My expenses consisted mainly of room and board charges, which amounted to $165 a month. The rest of the money was supposed to go toward the purchase of stationary, clothes, shoes, and food on weekends. Many of my boarding housemates managed to get by on only $250 a month; I was very lucky when it came to finances. However, rather than buying the things I was supposed to buy with the money left over after paying for room and board, the funds went toward my gambling habit.

Pachinko is a Japanese gambling device resembling a vertical pinball machine, but with automatic payoffs like a gambling slot machine. Pachinko was, and continues to be, very popular in Japan. Gambling for cash is illegal, but the widespread popularity of low-stakes pachinko in Japanese society enabled a legal loophole that allowed it to exist.

As a college student in Japan, I never spent money on clothes, shoes, stationary, or a haircut. Usually, I allocated $30 for food on weekends. I spent the remainder of what my parents sent me on pachinko. Sometimes, I burned through most of my food money well before I was to receive my next cash allotment from my parents. In those instances, I purchased a *korokke* (a Japanese potato croquette) at a store and went to a restaurant where I ordered a bowl of rice. I ate the korokke at the restaurant since they provided a glass of water free of charge and allowed me to use their chopsticks. It was easy to tell that the waitress was not happy with what I was doing, but I managed to sustain myself this way.

My parents never knew that I had a pachinko gambling habit or that I behaved in such an embarrassing manner. I was just young, crazy, and enjoying college life. I now regret that I wasted my parents' hard-earned money.

Kicked Out!

The owner of our boarding house began a relationship with one of our housemates, and no one liked it. I was the one who was the most vocal about the affair, and consequently, she asked me to leave.

By that time, I had made up my mind to go to college in America, although I had not shared my plans with my parents yet. I returned to Nagano to retrieve my car and started living with four of my friends, bouncing from one friend's room to another. Each friend had a tiny space, about 100 square feet, which the two of us shared for a while.

Finally, I moved into a nice house with another friend. It was a rental home he shared with his mother. She worked as a registered nurse and had moved from Kumamoto so her son could attend school. They were very nice people and we got along well. She cooked a nice dinner for us every night and never asked for a penny for rent. They let me stay at the house until I quit college a few months later.

Big Fight with My Parents

In 1948, a holiday known as *Seijin no Hi* (Coming of Age Day) was established to celebrate and encourage all those who reached the age of maturity (20 years old). Until 2000, the holiday was held every year on January 15. In 2000, as a result of the Happy Monday System, Coming of Age Day was changed to the second Monday in January.

In Nagano, the celebration was held at the City Hall, and it was a big deal. It was also an opportunity to see old classmates whom I had not seen for several years. I went back to my parents' house on January 14 to attend the celebration. Normally, men dressed in a suit and tie and women wore a very expensive kimono, which their parents purchased for this event. I, on the other hand, was a true non-conformist. The day before the celebration, I told my parents that I would dress in my usual hippie attire. Naturally, my parents were extremely upset, and I understood why. I was their only child at this point, and they would be very embarrassed when their neighbors saw me dressing like that for such a momentous occasion. The neighbors would probably have assumed that my parents could not afford to buy me a nice suit and tie.

My parents knew me well and realized that I would not back down, so they gave in. I attended the ceremony with two of my best friends, who were dressed very nicely, like everyone else. When we arrived at City

Hall, about three hundred people had already assembled, most of whom I knew. Some of them asked me why I had dressed that way, and I responded by saying that I did not want to dress like everyone else.

While sitting with my friends, I was approached by a television station reporter who wanted to interview me about the ceremony. During the interview, I told her that I didn't think it was right to mandate that people wear expensive clothes during the ceremony, particularly the women, since some of their kimonos cost upwards of $1,000. Some parents really could not afford such extravagances. Somehow they managed to scrape up the money to buy expensive kimonos for their daughters so they would not be embarrassed or forced to stay home during the event. When the reporter heard what I had to say, she walked away. I had not told her what she wanted to hear.

ix. My Coming of Age ceremony outfit, Nagano, Japan

x. With one of my motorcycles, Nagano

Return to Nagano

1972

Quitting College

Sometime in February 1972, I called my parents and told them that I was coming home to look for a job. I told them I wanted to save money, then go to college in the U.S.

They were very upset that I made this decision without consulting them first. However, they had to accept my choice as I was very stubborn. One week later, I was back living at my parents' house while I searched for a job.

My First Factory Job

With my cousin's help, I found a job at a nearby factory. I cleaned cylinder heads of engines for snowmobiles after they were cast. I did well on the job and people liked me. Like my mother, I did everything with speed and efficiency. However, I wasn't happy with the pay I was receiving. I commuted to my job on my motorcycle and only earned $15 a day. Sometimes, I got so depressed that I stopped by the Chikuma River on my way home and cried, thinking about how long it was going to take to save up enough money to go to college in the U.S. I had to find a different job.

Human Waste Tank Serviceman

In those days, the majority of households in Japan were not hooked up to *gesui* (public sewer systems). Most households had special tanks that collected the human waste. These tanks were cleaned out on a monthly basis.

On my way home from work one day, I called a few companies that cleaned the human waste from these tanks and hauled it to a treatment plant. The owner of one company asked me to come and work for him the next day, and he offered me $35 a day. I was elated. This was a substantial increase compared to the $15 a day I was earning at the snowmobile factory.

I quit my factory job that day and eagerly went to work for my new employer. Why would I be so eager to work for a human waste tank cleaning company, you might ask? At that time, I was willing to do anything that would help me save a considerable sum of money.

On my first day, I was introduced to three of the company's employees. Two were in their late fifties, and one was just twenty-two. I also met the owner's girlfriend, who was in her sixties. The young employee was so embarrassed to be working for this type of company that he hid his identity by wearing a pair of dark sunglasses when he was out in the field. Japan was, and still is, a hierarchical society in many aspects. The social status of a human waste tank serviceman was at the very bottom of the tier, even though the pay was rather good.

I was assigned a vacuum truck with a two-ton capacity holding tank. The truck was equipped with a seventy-five-foot suction hose with an outside diameter of three inches. The hose was wound on top of the holding tank. The newer trucks had an automatic hose retractor on top of the tank. My truck was older, so I had to manually wind the long hose on top of the holding tank or drag it on the road if the next tank that needed servicing was nearby. On the side of the truck was a drain hose measuring five inches in diameter. I also had a six-foot-long metal rod with a handle on one end and a four-by-four-inch metal plate welded to the other end, which I used for mixing.

I later learned that the owner of the company never did any work. He assigned his girlfriend to accompany me until I could remember all the houses that had to be serviced each month. My route included 3,000 human waste tanks. The owner promised that he would increase my pay from $35 a day to $40 a day if I remembered all 3,000 houses to visit. The girlfriend's main job was to direct me to where I needed to go. I was given a pair of rubber gloves, but she refused to wear any gloves at all.

I still vividly recall the first house we visited. The girlfriend opened the human waste tank cover to reveal a mound of feces resembling Mount Fuji, the highest mountain in Japan, surrounded by a urine moat. Actually, the sight was not as bad as I had expected. She instructed me to get the metal rod from the truck and stir the contents of the tank, which enabled the hose to suck up the mixture more easily into the truck's holding tank. I followed her instructions and rigorously stirred the mixture. Amazingly, there was no foul smell to contend with. I unwound the hose on top of the holding tank and carried it to the human waste tank. I then opened the suction inlet valve and moved the accelerator lever to increase the engine's speed and raise the suction power of the hose.

It took approximately ten minutes to clean the tank. Once finished, I rewound the hose on top of the holding tank, placed the soiled tip of the hose into a plastic cup, and moved on to the next house.

A Vacuum Truck Driver's Daily Routine

Each morning, my mother prepared two large *onigiri* (rice balls) for my lunch. I left our house around 7:40 a.m. and drove to work in my car. I arrived by 8 a.m., making me the last employee to come to work.

The owner's girlfriend and I departed shortly thereafter and visited a little over one hundred houses a day, on average. After servicing twenty-five houses, the holding tank reached its capacity and needed to be drained. I drove the truck to the waste treatment center about five miles away.

There was a specific technique we had to use when emptying the holding tank. An eight-inch hole was encased in concrete on the ground at the treatment center. I had to place the tip of my truck's drain hose into this concrete-encased hole and applied positive pressure to the holding tank to promote faster drainage. During the draining process, I was required to place my foot firmly over the drain hose to keep it in place.

While I was waiting for the drainage to finish, I washed off the tip of the suction hose and the truck itself. Then I returned to work. I visited the treatment facility five times each day, returned to the company around 3 p.m., washed my face and hands, and drove back home. I was always the first employee to return to the company because of my speed and efficiency.

Working as a human waste tank serviceman was very challenging during the hot and humid Nagano summers. Oftentimes, the temperature hovered around 90 degrees Fahrenheit and the humidity reached 90 percent.

The Fastest Human Waste Tank Cleaner in Nagano

If there had been a human waste tank cleaning competition, I would have been the winner. I always ran everywhere, and I mastered all the fast and efficient cleaning techniques. For example, some of the apartment buildings on my route had their waste tank covers arranged next to each other. With the metal stirring rod in my hand, I opened the first tank cover, stirred the contents within it, and placed the suction hose inside the tank. While the hose was suctioning the contents of the first tank, I ran over and removed the covers from the remaining tanks. I returned to the first tank, finished cleaning it, quickly moved to the next tank, and so on. When finished, I wound the hose on top of the holding tank and drove to the next building.

If anyone had witnessed me cleaning the tanks in those days, they probably would have thought I was peculiar. But I really did not care what people thought about me as I was doing my job. However, I have to admit that being fast did have its drawbacks. I always ran as I pulled the long, heavy suction hose through the narrow paths between the houses and gardens. On a few occasions, I broke some bonsai pots and other things placed outside by the homeowners. Fortunately, no one ever complained.

One cold morning, I was running as usual while pulling the long suction hose. Its tip was dripping with the waste material from the previous location. I ran past a fourteen-inch-diameter pan that was outside with some rice cakes soaking in water in it. As I carried the hose over the pan, three small drops of waste found their way onto the water in the pan. Once they hit the water, they spread like ink drops. I was mortified, but I kept moving and finished the job at hand.

Hose Attack

After I had been on the job for a month, I was teamed up with an older man in addition to the owner's girlfriend. On the third day, the three of us were working together and parked the truck in front of an alleyway between two houses. It was a narrow lane, only about five feet wide.

The older gentleman unwound the entire length of the hose from the top of the holding tank and proceeded into the alleyway. When he was halfway down the alley, the owner's girlfriend opened the valve of the seventy-five-foot suction hose he was carrying. Unfortunately, she made the mistake of depressing the positive pressure switch, which sent the contents of the half-full holding tank through the nozzle of the hose with tremendous velocity. I watched helplessly as the older man struggled like a novice firefighter as he tried to gain control of the hose. It danced violently in his arms and sprayed the white walls of the houses and the alleyway in brown excrement.

After about ten seconds had passed, the woman realized she had made a mistake, but it was ten seconds too late. The damage had already been done. I do not recall whether there was any odor, but everything had been covered by waste. We borrowed a water hose from one of the homeowners to clean up the mess. He was much too astonished to be angry. It took us almost two hours to restore order and cleanliness.

Waste Shower

After two months, I was able to do the job on my own without the help of the owner's girlfriend or the older man. I finally knew all 3,000 houses I had to service, and my salary rose from $35 to $40 a day.

One day, I brought the truck to the treatment center to empty the tank. The center resembled a giant carport with a roof cover. There were two drain holes encased in cement at the facility. The drivers checked in at a small office with a large glass window adjacent to the carport.

While I was draining the holding tank of my truck, with my foot securely placed on the drain hose, another company's vacuum truck pulled in, and the driver began emptying the contents of his truck's holding tank. He began washing off his truck but forgot to secure the drain hose with his foot. Within a minute or so, I felt as though someone had dumped a bucketful of human waste over my entire body. And it did not end there; excrement from the out-of-control hose continued to douse the area for another five seconds.

Realizing his mistake, the driver quickly shut off the drain valve, but it was too little, too late. The ground, roof covering, windows, white walls, and I were all covered in putrid excrement. I was wearing a baseball cap, but human excrement covered me from head to toe, making me resemble a creature from a low-budget horror film. I was so shocked to see myself in that condition that I did not have the will to get angry at the driver.

I washed my body with a water hose as much as possible and returned to my company, where I shampooed my hair twice before driving home. I was scheduled to visit friends in Saitama that night and did not have time to take a bath at home.

When I arrived at my friend's place, we started playing mahjong. At some point, I ran my fingers through my hair, but my fingers became entangled in something I did not recognize. As I forced my fingers through my hair,

I realized that there was a chunk of white bathroom tissue stuck in between my fingers. I suppose I had not adequately shampooed my hair after the waste shower. When I explained what had happened to my friends, they ordered me to get out.

Lost and Found

One day, I was servicing a tank that was oddly located inside the house and behind the front door. While I was cleaning, an old man stood beside me. He anxiously watched me work like a dog waiting for its master to return home. I thought it was rather odd until I realized what had happened.

He had dropped his wallet into the tank and was waiting to see if I would find it. I did pull up the wallet, cleaned it off, and handed it to him. He was so excited that if he had had a tail, he would have wagged it. I cannot recall if he thanked me.

Finding things that people dropped into the tank, whether accidentally or deliberately, was just part of the job. The most common thing that people dropped into the tank unintentionally were bathroom slippers. Japanese people typically wear a different pair of slippers in the bathroom. If they have a squat toilet, they place one leg on each side of the opening in order to squat down. In the process of moving one leg over the hole to place it on the other side, one of the slippers sometimes slips off and falls into the hole. As a little boy, I dropped my slippers into the tank a few times, but I picked them up and washed them off for fear of getting scolded.

The most common item dropped into the tank intentionally were sanitary pads. These items gave me a lot of trouble when I was cleaning the tanks.

They clogged up the suction hose, and I had trouble dislodging them. At times, the pressure created by a sanitary pad lodged in the tip of the suction hose caused waste to spew out all over the place when the item finally dislodged itself and went through the hose. I learned a few techniques to prevent this from happening, but occasionally I got hit in the face with waste. Getting hit with waste did not cause me to panic. I casually wiped my face with my sleeve and continued working.

Don't Mess With a Man Holding a Dirty Suction Hose

There were times when I was forced to stretch the suction hose across the entire surface of the road while I was working. Typically, no one complained, and most people patiently waited until I finished the job.

One day, while I was servicing a house in a subdivision, I noticed that an expensive looking black car had stopped. I glared at the driver, imploring him to wait and not to run over the hose. He was an impatient individual, apparently, and only waited for about a minute before he drove over it. I approached his car with my stirring rod and dirty hose tip, shouting obscenities. As I got closer, I recognized that he looked like a stereotypical *yakuza* (a member of a Japanese organized crime syndicate), but I did not care. I had something that I was sure he was afraid of, a hose that would cover him from head to toe in human waste. If that had not worked, I would have pulverized him with my soiled metal stirring rod.

There is no worse threat than the wrath of an outraged man who can shower someone with human excrement. The driver apologized to me and left.

Gender Bender

My typical work clothes consisted of a baseball cap, sunglasses, a tight shirt, a tight pair of pants, and rubber boots. I wore the sunglasses not to protect my eyes but to look cool.

When I wore brightly colored shirts, people often mistook me for a woman. Several times, I encountered a group of elementary school students arguing about whether I was a man or a woman.

As I was working one day, an old man came out of his house and handed me a tip. He said, "Thank you very much for your excellent work, young lady." I took the tip and thanked him, but told him that he was mistaken about my gender. In all honesty, I did not care if people mistook me for a woman.

A Misconception About My Job

There were days when I would come home so tired and worn out that I could barely crawl up the stairs to my bedroom. I was only twenty years old at the time. In addition to working full time, I was taking karate lessons three times a week and tutoring my friend's cousin twice a week, driving ten miles round trip. I was often too exhausted to take a bath. People asked me whether my line of work left a foul smell on my body that a shower or a bath could not remove. The answer is no.

Although I was very busy and tired every day, my motivation to save enough money to attend college in the U.S. kept me going. I focused solely on this goal and did not care about the negative comments people made about my job.

Added Benefits

Unlike gardeners, mailmen, or pool boys, I did not score big with the ladies as I was a human waste tank serviceman. But I did get a lot of tips. In those days, people tipped me with money or cigarettes. I often received up to $50 in cash and thirty packs of cigarettes each month. During the nine months I worked at this job, I never had to purchase my own cigarettes.

Ogling on the Job

As I drove the vacuum truck around the streets of Nagano, I combated boredom in various ways. One was to take advantage of my high vantage point. Since a truck is much higher than a car, I often had clear views of women in cars wearing miniskirts. When sitting at a stop light, I found myself ogling.

Searching for a U.S. College to Attend

While I was working as a human waste tank serviceman, I actively looked for a college in California that would accept me. I applied to ten institutions. Some of them were junior colleges, and others were community colleges. I even found a few that did not charge foreign students for tuition. However, since I had not taken TOEFL, a standardized test to measure the English language ability of non-native speakers wishing to enroll in English-speaking universities, no college was willing to accept me.

I managed to find a company in Tokyo that, for a fee, would find a school for me that did not require the TOEFL test. The company suggested that

I apply to Humphreys College (currently known as Humphreys University) in Stockton, California. At the time, Humphreys was a private, two-year college.

I obtained my F1 student visa from the American Embassy in Tokyo and was about to realize my dream.

Going to California

I saved about $9,000 by working as a human waste tank serviceman for nine months. It was a considerable sum of money 50 years ago. I left Japan on December 17, 1972, bound for California.

xi. Circa 1973

Stockton

December 1972 – August 1973

Meeting Mark

I arrived at San Francisco International Airport on December 17, 1972, and was twenty years old. I found a cheap room at a downtown hotel for the night, as I was planning to leave for Stockton the next day. But I caught a bad cold and extended my stay in San Francisco for two more days.

After the two days had passed, I still felt sick. But I managed to get to the Greyhound bus terminal. Since I was unsure which bus to take, I asked a young man standing next to me to point me toward the bus bound for Stockton. He immediately picked up my suitcase and asked me to follow him. He walked so fast that I could barely keep up with him. When we reached the bus, he turned to me and said, "Here is your bus. I am going to Stockton, too."

We sat next to each other on the bus, and I learned that his name was Mark. He was my age, and he was in San Francisco for a routine monthly exam at the hospital. I asked him to call me Mickey and explained why I was traveling to Stockton. We arrived at the Stockton Greyhound bus terminal, and his girlfriend, Nancy, was waiting to pick us up. Mark asked Nancy to drive us to Humphreys College.

When we got there, we saw a number of apartment buildings under the same management right next to the college. We met with an apartment manager, who helped me find an apartment to move into right away. Afterward, Mark and Nancy took me to a K-Mart, where I purchased a few inexpensive household items including bedding, utensils, pots and pans, and some canned foods. The yellow blanket I bought was so cheap that I woke up every morning covered with yellow lint.

The following day, Mark and Nancy returned to help me shop for food. There was a Safeway grocery store just a couple of blocks from my school. I was amused by the fact that the grocery store was larger than the school.

Mark and I became good friends after this. He introduced me to his friends, his brother, Bill, and he took me to many different places. As I was sitting in his garage one day, Mark fashioned a belt buckle for me out of wood. He had excellent woodworking skills, and I still have the buckle; it has been fifty years since he gave it to me. I recently got in touch with Mark and learned that he and his wife, Nancy, were enjoying their retirement. We had not talked for over fifteen years, and I am glad I was able to connect with them again.

The Yamaha

With Mark's help, I purchased a used 1966 Yamaha YDS-3, a two-stroke, two-cylinder motorcycle, from one of his friends. I had an international driver's license that allowed me to drive a motorcycle or a car in the United States. Before making the purchase, I took the bike for a test ride. As I rode away, Mark and his friend shouted something behind my back, but I could not understand what they were saying over the noise of the motorcycle's engine. I took the bike through the streets of a residential area in Stockton. When I returned, Mark shouted that I was riding on the wrong side of the street. I did not know what he was talking about. Later,

I realized that Americans drive on the opposite side of the street to the Japanese. Luckily, I had not encountered any traffic during my test ride.

This motorcycle was my only mode of transportation. I rode it everywhere in all types of weather. One day, in the middle of winter, I took the bike on the freeway at speeds over 90 miles per hour. I wore a pair of jeans, but I had no goggles, so my eyes were teary in the cold. It was a frightening journey as I could hardly see anything.

Sometimes I rode my motorcycle barefoot with my guitar strapped to my back. I was a hippie wannabe and often wondered around without shoes. Stockton experienced very hot summers, and the temperatures easily reached over 100 degrees Fahrenheit. One summer day, I was riding my bike barefoot with my guitar on my back as usual. I stopped at a red light and had to place my feet on the scorching ground. The pavement was so hot that I could not keep my feet on it for longer than three seconds. I must have resembled a dancing octopus to passersby, who saw me raising and lowering my feet alternately on the hot asphalt every three seconds. I knew someone who had suffered from huge blisters on the bottom of both feet after walking barefoot on extremely hot asphalt. I was lucky that did not happen to me. Sometimes, I scraped my toes on the ground while I was cornering my bike without wearing shoes.

Other Students at Humphreys College

Since Humphreys College divided the school year into quarters instead of semesters, I started college in January 1973. Humphreys College was a small, private college, and I only saw a few hundred students on campus during the day. The school offered law and other classes at night.

I met another Japanese student that year. He was from Tokyo and one year older than I. He called himself Kei. Later, we were joined by another Japanese student who called himself Max. Max had hitchhiked across Europe before coming to the United States. He planned to become an actor in Japan, and he constantly coached us on how to act in certain situations. As time wore on, his behavior became intolerable. Kei and I started picking on him incessantly, to the point where he got scared and left Stockton. About fifteen years ago, I saw him on Japanese television. He had become an actor and comedian. I was impressed with his determination to realize his dream.

For our second quarter at Humphreys College, Kei and I wanted to take a precalculus class. We both attained nearly perfect scores on the placement test. On the first day of class, our professor advised us that we would not need to attend class as long as we submitted our homework. We both received A grades in precalculus at the end of the quarter.

I also took an English 101 class, and I was the only foreign student among the twenty-five native speakers in the class. As our professor was returning our test papers to us, he remarked to the class that I had attained the highest score. This was unbelievable to me. How could a foreign kid outscore students who were born and raised in the United States?

I also did well in the computer and accounting courses but not as well in the history class. Compared to my college life in Japan, I studied a little harder in the U.S.

Obtaining a U.S. Driver's License

When the time came for me to obtain my driver's and motorcycle licenses in the U.S., Mark drove me to the Department of Motor Vehicles. As he was helping me complete the application, he asked me to look into his eyes. I was puzzled by this request, but I did as he wished. Then I heard him say "hazel," to himself as he jotted something down on the form. I did not understand what he meant until several years later. I have never encountered another Japanese person with hazel eyes. However, when I was a junior high school student, one of my fellow students persistently told me that I had green eyes. I never paid attention to it until years later. I learned that there are two main types of hazel eyes: those with brown as the dominant iris color and those with green as the dominant color. While all hazel eyes have a combination of green and brown colors, the difference in dominant colors is why hazel eyes can appear mostly green or mostly brown. I realized that my eyes appeared greenish under bright sunlight, which really surprised me.

At the Department of Motor Vehicles, I passed the written test with flying colors. The motorcycle riding test mainly involved riding my motorbike for several blocks around the DMV facility. When I returned, the examiner told me that I passed the test. It struck me as rather strange; the requirements in Japan were far stricter. The vehicle driving test was equally easy. The examiner asked me to drive my car for three blocks around the DMV facility. I was not required to parallel park or anything else. I passed without a problem.

My First U.S. Car

My first car in the U.S. was a 1965 Chevy Impala SS, and I purchased it for $500. At the time, I had no idea that this car would become such a classic collectible. These days (in 2023), an Impala in excellent shape can sell for tens of thousands of dollars.

Back then, I was not the car afficionado I am today, so I did not realize my Impala was missing its air cleaner filter. I routinely drove that car on the freeway at speeds over 80 miles per hour. Within three months, the engine consumed about a quart of oil every 500 miles. Soon, I replaced the Impala with a yellow 1966 Mustang with a 289 Windsor V8 engine, which cost me $100 more than the Impala did.

Speed Demon

I had quite a lead foot in those days. I received four speeding tickets in seven months and was on probation for one year. Fortunately, I drove responsibly for the duration of the year and got let off the hook.

Party Culture

I met a tall, blonde, heavyset student named Bill. We lived in the same apartment complex. His 1957 Chevy Bel Air station wagon was his pride and joy. I thought it was ugly.

Every Friday and Saturday, he had a party at his place, which many people attended. I was one of them. We did not do anything crazy or delve into drugs, but there were heavy drinking and loud music. The drinks of choice back then were beer and the one-gallon finger-ringed jug of cheap red wine produced by Gallo. I did not drink, so I sipped orange juice at these parties.

One of the regulars at Bill's parties was a young Mexican American girl named Marissa. She offered to marry me so I could obtain a green card. I was unfamiliar with the immigration laws and politely declined her offer. Later on, I realized that if I had married her, I could have saved my parents thousands of dollars in tuition payments. Tuition was higher for out-of-state students, and being on a student visa put me in that category. I was too young and naïve to even consider that Marissa would have committed marriage fraud and taken advantage of me.

My First Sexual Encounter in the U.S.

In school, I met a twenty-something Italian farm worker named Mateo. He had blue eyes, blonde hair, and a small stature. One day, he started bragging about having sex with a Mexican lady in his Datsun truck. He told me how easy it was to get her to have sex with him, so I asked him to set me up on a date with her. He agreed.

We were scheduled to go out on Saturday. I picked her up at her place and we drove to the restaurant where we were going to have dinner. While we were waiting for the waitress to come and take our order, I had the urge to smoke a cigarette. I had placed a box of cigarettes and a wine-colored box with gold trim containing three condoms in my upper shirt pocket. I attempted to remove the box of cigarettes from my pocket, and the box of condoms came out too. It landed on top of the cigarette box, right on the table where she could see it. I quickly picked up the box of condoms and placed it back inside my shirt pocket. But it was too late.

She saw it and kept questioning me as to what it was. I repeatedly told her that it was nothing, but I think she knew and understood my intentions.

After dinner we went to a drive-in theater, but I have no recollection of what the movie was.

Moving Out

To save some money, I moved out of my first apartment and into a house owned by an old lady.

I rented a single room and was given the privilege of using the kitchen when needed. I earned a few extra dollars every now and then by helping her with her gardening. I supplemented my income further by helping other old widows in the neighborhood with their gardening as well.

Arrested!

Mark taught me how to make bracelets and necklaces out of horseshoe nails and wire using a pair of round nose pliers. I brought my creations to the flea markets but did not sell many. I sold some of the items I handcrafted to various ladies through some friends.

I needed to replenish my supplies, so I went to Payless Super Drug Store. I found everything I needed at the store, but I was suddenly overcome by the urge to procure some of these items free of charge, which is called theft. I had never pilfered anything before in my life.

Nervous and indecisive, I paced back and forth in the same aisle, unwittingly drawing attention to myself. I approached the cashier and paid for the cheaper item while I pocketed the more expensive item. It was totally unnecessary as I had enough money to pay for everything. Had I done so, the entire purchase would have been less than $3.

I had an uneasy feeling as I walked out of the store, and I thought that someone was following me. Sure enough, two store employees approached me from behind and grabbed both my hands. They led me back to the drug store, into an office upstairs, and telephoned the police. As the police officer questioned me, I became transfixed by the big gun hanging in his holster.

I was so completely devasted by this incident that strange, unexplainable thoughts about using the gun on myself crossed my mind. I feared that I would be arrested, thrown into jail, and eventually deported back to Japan. I actually believed that my dream of living in America would be destroyed by this compulsive act.

However, to my surprise, the officer released me after handing me a pink ticket and telling me to appear in court on a certain date. Although I felt somewhat relieved, I knew I was not out of the woods yet. The judge could possibly put me in jail and report me to immigration for deportation.

I was barely able to contain my anxiety when I arrived home. With no one else to talk to, I told my landlady what had happened. She calmly informed me that it was not a big deal, and I should go to court and pay the appropriate fine. Her comment really helped ease my mind.

Recently, when I got in touch with Mark, I told him about this incident in Stockton. He laughed and joked, "You went to Payless to buy things, right? But you wanted to *pay less,* as the store's name implied. I guess by not paying for an item, you really couldn't have paid any less."

My Day in Court

A few weeks after receiving the pink ticket, I went to the Municipal Court in downtown Stockton. Upon entering the courtroom, I noticed that there were a lot of elderly people there. As I waited to be called, I watched and listened to the judge as he imposed sentences for misdemeanor charges for petty theft to the elderly people.

Finally, my name was called. The judge explained to me why I was being charged with a misdemeanor for petty theft. I listened to him and admitted my guilt. He gave me a fine of $60. Before dismissing me, he asked, "Now you are not going to do this again, are you?" In response, I proudly proclaimed, "Yes sir!" As soon as those words left my mouth, I heard laughter behind me, and I wondered whether or not I had said the wrong thing. The judge asked me again, "You are not going to do it again, are you?" I assumed I did not respond loud enough the first time and answered "Yes" in an even louder voice. This puzzled the judge and the laughter behind me was even louder than before. He asked me the same question once again and I responded in the same manner, but much louder than the second time. An agonizing look came over the judge's face. He finally gave up and released me.

In Japan, if you are asked a question like the one the judge asked me, you always respond with *hai* (yes). That day, I learned an enduring lesson about crime and the English language.

My First Girlfriend

During my second quarter at Humphreys College, a cute girl working at a take-out hamburger shop caught my eye. She was a petite, blue-eyed blonde. I visited the shop three times before I worked up the courage to ask her out. To my surprise, she agreed to go out with me and gave me her phone number.

On my way home, fireworks were exploding inside my head, and I was ready to burst with excitement. We went to see a movie on our first date and hit it off well, but the relationship ended after just two months. I had not realized the challenges of dating a virgin.

Travels to Lake Tahoe with Kei

My friend, Kei, wanted to go to Lake Tahoe to gamble, and he encouraged me to go with him. Little did I know that this first gambling trip would lead me down the disastrous road to a gambling addiction.

Lake Tahoe is approximately 135 miles from Stockton, and we went there once a month. Sometimes I made the trip alone. On our first visit we each won $50 playing the slot machines. We returned to Lake Tahoe two weeks later, but we were not as lucky this time. We both lost our money. I learned how to play blackjack, but I seldom made any money.

A Nurse's Aide with Interesting Patients

After my second quarter at Humphreys College ended, a friend helped me secure a position as a nurse's aide at a local convalescent hospital during the summer vacation. I worked the evening shift from 3 p.m. to 11 p.m. I took this job primarily because I wanted to make money, not because I was interested in caring for people.

My manager was a registered nurse in her forties. She was tall, loud, competent, and nice. She really liked me because I was fast and efficient. Working at a convalescent hospital, I came across people of all types.

A Patient in a Vegetative State

When a person is in a vegetative state, they are awake but show no signs of awareness. My encounter with a seventeen-year-old patient in a vegetative state left me questioning how aware he really was.

The patient had suffered brain damage after a car accident, placed in the hospital, and entrusted to our care. One day, as a young nurse and I were cleaning his body, he became aroused. Our natural reaction was to laugh. We weren't aware that someone who was in this condition would be capable of becoming aroused.

Sadly, six months after I had left the hospital, I learned that this young man had passed away.

A Rabbit in his Former Life

Approximately fifty percent of the patients were incapable of going to the bathroom on their own. Consequently, we had to change their linen diapers. This task was not difficult or problematic for me since I had already worked as a human waste tank serviceman in Japan.

One patient in his early eighties was completely paralyzed. Since he could not move on his own, we had to turn his body regularly to prevent him from developing bed sores.

When I changed his diaper, I swore that he had to have been a rabbit in his former life. His excrement resembled that of a rabbit. Each piece was 1/3 inch in diameter, almost perfectly round, and there were about ten pieces in the soiled diaper at all times.

The Mexican Amputee

Lorenzo was in his late seventies and of Mexican heritage. He was blind, and doctors had amputated both legs below the knees. But that didn't mean he wasn't dangerous. He was very combative; he punched and kicked his caretakers while swearing at them in Spanish.

I had to be careful when placing him in a wheelchair and taking him to the dining room. He caught me off guard several times and punched me in the face.

The Neurosyphilis Patient

Another patient was a tall, skinny Chinese man in his early eighties. He had a peculiar habit of tapping the top of his head with his right palm when he walked down the hallway. He always had a bewildered look on his face. I was told that he was suffering from neurosyphilis, a condition that impacts the brain about ten to twenty years after a person is infected with syphilis.

He managed to escape our watchful eyes and went outside in the middle of one of the hottest summer days. He wasn't wearing anything on his feet, which got burned pretty badly, causing huge blisters.

The MVP

There was another Mexican patient in our care. He was in his seventies and partially paralyzed. He had a special gift, which he revealed to me three times.

When he was on his side facing the window, he removed his diaper, grabbed a handful of his excrement, and molded it into a ball about twice the size of a golf ball. He then threw it at the window, where it landed perfectly on the window ledge. He never missed his target. Three times I witnessed three excrement balls sitting next to each other on the window ledge.

At some point, I became convinced that he was an MVP pitcher for the Mexican professional baseball league in his younger days.

A Scene Like a Horror Film

A Caucasian man in his late seventies was hospitalized with late-stage lung cancer. He was under my care for about two weeks.

One night at around 10 p.m., I was amazed when I entered his room to check on him. Nearly all of the walls were covered with his blood. His room looked like a scene out of a B-rated horror film. The most mystifying aspect was that he was still in bed. I could not fathom how he had coughed up blood and spewed it all over the walls while he remained in his bed.

I believe he passed away the next day.

The Patient with Alzheimer's Disease

Our third Mexican patient was in his early eighties and suffering from Alzheimer's disease. He was a small man with a pacemaker implanted in his chest. He had trouble remembering things, and he hardly spoke.

A urinal was attached to the hand railing next to his bed, but he refused to use it. After numerous attempts to entice him to use the urinal had failed, I lost my patience and asked him to use the urinal, or I would become upset with him. I later regretted using such strong language. I found him dead, with his mouth gaping open, during my rounds the following night.

After six weeks of working at this hospital, I found work at another convalescent hospital in the same town.

Another Hospital

I worked the earlier shift at the second convalescent hospital. My day began at 7 a.m. and ended at 3 p.m. When I came in, I pushed the meal tray cart through the halls and distributed breakfast trays to each patient. I fed those who were unable to feed themselves.

The one aspect of this job that I absolutely loathed was cleaning the patients' dentures. I cleaned human waste tanks in Japan, but cleaning dentures really sickened me.

After breakfast, I made sure all the patients had a bowel movement. As most patients were confined in their beds, many suffered from constipation. I learned three methods to help relieve their suffering:

lukewarm water enemas, suppositories, and my middle finger with lots of Vaseline for lubricant.

Speed and Efficiency

No matter what type of work I was involved in, I had one trait that always carried over naturally; I was the fastest and most efficient worker. Dealing with patients in the convalescent hospital was no exception. I found that helping relieve them of their constipation was very time consuming if I prepared a lukewarm water enema or relied on a suppository to do the job. It was much faster and more efficient when I used my gloved finger and lots of Vaseline.

The suppositories were always locked in a cabinet, but I managed to steal one and experimented with it myself. I wanted to know what my patients endured while being treated with a suppository. The medication worked almost instantaneously, but I still thought my finger was superior. I regarded myself as the "human plumber" while working at the second convalescent hospital.

However, my speed and efficiency worked against me in this instance. My career as a nurse's aide came to an abrupt end after just three weeks.

One morning, the nurse I was assisting asked me to change a patient's diaper, clean his dentures, and wash his face. I finished my assigned tasks and returned to the nurses' station in less than five minutes. Seeing me back so quickly, the head nurse approached me and asked me if I had completed all the tasks the nurse assigned to me. I nodded. She grew angry with me and told me I could not have done everything in less than five minutes.

She marched into the patient's room to check if I had done everything, and I accompanied her. To her surprise, she learned that I was telling the truth, but she still implied that I must not have taken the time to take care of the patient. Later that day, when my shift ended, I was fired.

I realized then that speed and efficiency were not trusted in the convalescent hospital.

Burning Through Money

I arrived in the United States with $9,000 in my pocket, but it did not last long. After paying for tuition and rent, what I spent on food, supplies, and my gambling habit quickly burned through my savings.

I had no choice but to ask my parents to help me. They agreed to do so, and in addition to paying my tuition, they promised to send me $1,500 every three months.

Modesto

September 1973 – March 1975

Modesto Junior College

During summer vacation, I applied to Modesto Junior College, a public community college established in 1921. Even though it charged foreign students a higher tuition fee, I was happy to be accepted for the fall semester. In late August, I crammed everything I owned into my Impala and moved into a house owned by a retired doctor and his wife.

The elderly couple rented rooms to foreign students; an Iranian student and a Chinese student lived there when I arrived. The three of us did not talk much. However, I made a lot of new friends in school. Many of them were foreign students like me, but the majority of my friends were female American students. Similar to my previous living arrangement, I was allowed to use the kitchen, but I never cooked in that house.

I was a full-time student at Modesto Junior College, but because I was still lamenting my breakup with the blonde girl in Stockton, I did not do well academically during my first semester. To my horror, the school placed me on academic probation.

Black Belt

I met a Japanese student from Hokkaido at Modesto Junior College. He wanted to become a rancher and worked as a ranch hand while attending college. He had a second-degree black belt in judo and taught judo at the college.

He knew that I was accomplished in judo even though I did not have a belt. One day, he invited me to his judo class and introduced me to his students as someone with a black belt. Afterward, the unthinkable happened. One of his students challenged me to a match. He was 5'10" and weighed around 180 pounds. I, on the other hand, was only 140 pounds at the time. To make matters worse, he had a brown belt, just one rank below a black belt.

My friend was amused by this and gestured to me to accept the student's challenge. My back was up against a wall, so to speak, so I accepted. As we began the match, I could tell that the student did not want to be thrown to the mat by someone with a black belt. He used a defensive stance throughout the match to prevent this from happening. Fortunately, after five minutes, my friend declared the match a draw. It was a moral victory for both of us.

When my friend was getting ready to return to Japan, he gave me his black belt as a memento.

Karate Practice

While I was a human waste vacuum truck driver, I took karate lessons three times a week. When I moved to Modesto, I practiced karate in my own unique way. In addition to throwing kicks and punches in the air, I kicked and punched various objects, mainly the trunks of the trees that lined the street in front of the house where I was renting a room. I did not bother wearing any protective gear, like gloves, when I went out battering the tree trunks.

Being a consummate showoff, I incorporated summersaults and backflips for showmanship while kicking and punching the helpless trees. My relentless and unorthodox methods of practicing karate resulted in my knuckles, particularly the ones on my right hand, becoming permanently deformed.

To strengthen my knuckles and wrists, I did handstands and walked on my knuckles on concrete surfaces. My toe strengthening exercises involved curling my toes in and walking on hard surfaces.

When I saw an orthopedic doctor several years ago, he asked me to walk on my toes across his office floor. I knew exactly what he wanted me to do; however, I really wanted to surprise him by doing my curled-toe walk. After witnessing my crazy act, he told me that no patient of his had ever done that before.

In those early days, my favorite thing to do was to break a piece of wood using my forehead. Each time I saw a piece of wood lying around, I got an urge to break it by holding it with my hands and striking it on my forehead. When I did this in front of people, they felt intimidated, which pleased me immensely. Once, I broke a dinner plate on my forehead and lacerated my skin.

One day, my humanities class at Modesto Junior College afforded me the opportunity to demonstrate my wood-breaking techniques. Usually, karate demonstrations involve breakable boards. I purchased one-inch-thick wooden boards from the lumber yard and cut them into ten pieces for my demonstration.

The Haircut

A Japanese student from Nagoya and I became very good friends while I attended Modesto Junior College. His name was Akira, and he was two years younger than I. He was renting a room from a very conservative but nice elderly woman. I visited him every day.

One day, we were hanging out in his room, and I told him that his hair was too long. Actually, his hair was just a little over an inch over the top of his ears, but I told him I would cut it for him. I had never cut anyone's hair before, and he showed some resistance when I shared that opinion with him. But eventually he relented and let me do it.

He got a new razor blade and handed it to me. I mischievously grabbed a two-inch section of his hair above his left ear and moved the razor blade downward at a seventy-degree angle. When it was all said and done, I was shocked to see such a large bundle of his hair in my hand. To make matters even worse, there was now one-inch bald spot above his ear.

As soon as I noticed the bald spot, I fell to the floor laughing hysterically. Akira panicked and ran into the bathroom. When he emerged, he was absolutely furious. He started screaming at me as tears welled up in his eyes. "What have you done?" he shouted. "What am I going to do?"

Somehow, I managed to calm him down and proceeded to finish cutting his hair, trying to make it appear more presentable. I did my best, but the bald spot was still visible. Rather than apologize, I said to him, "You should be happy that I did not slice your ear off. I call this the two-month special. Your hair will look perfect in two months!" He was distraught and asked, "Until then, what am I going to do?" We remained good friends despite this, and he even helped me with a photo shoot.

Akira owned a very nice Japanese camera, and I asked him if he would be willing to take some photos of me, which I turned into posters. He agreed, and we set up an area for the shoot in his backyard. I wore tight purple pants, a multi-color button-down shirt, and brown shoes. In some shots, I wore an ivy cap.

The photos Akira took turned out very well, but I had to select just one to make into a 24" X 36" poster. I could not afford to have full-color posters made, so I opted for five black and white posters. I gave these to the girls I knew, hoping that they would decorate their rooms with them. I never knew if any of them actually did.

Emi

One of the students Akira and I used to hang around with was Emi. She was a *hafu* (half Japanese and half Caucasian) and one year younger than I. Emi came from a wealthy family. Her American father lived in Japan and was engaged in dealing with antique Japanese swords. It was his dream for Emi to become a good tennis player, and he hired a professional tennis coach for her. In my opinion, Emi was not very talented when it came to tennis. She eventually quit playing.

The three of us spent a lot of time together hanging out, going to movies, and playing tennis. Emi briefly dated a Mexican guy named Gustavo, who was our age. When they broke up, she began spending more time with me.

xii. Photo taken by Akira

One night, she invited me to her house, which she shared with a young, attractive, blue-eyed blonde. The two of us studied together until 2 a.m. Since she did not want me to go home so late, she suggested I spend the night on the couch. I agreed.

Around 6 a.m., I was awakened by someone sneaking under my blanket and crawling up from my legs to my torso. I immediately recognized that it was Emi. I quickly became aroused when she started rubbing my legs with her feet. Before I knew it, we were doing the "no pants polka." I felt like a jockey riding a thoroughbred.

We were at a good gallop when, all of a sudden, I heard someone scream at the top of her lungs, "What the hell are you two monkeys doing over there?" It was her blonde roommate. As soon as we heard that, we got up and dressed at lightning speed.

After this incident, Emi tried to become more intimate with me. I did not want any part of it. It would have contradicted the American life I had always dreamed of. One day, when she came over to see me, I told her the truth. I said I was not ready for the kind of deep relationship that she wanted and suggested that we continue being friends. This was not what she wanted to hear. She started swearing at me using every Japanese expletive she knew and stormed out of my house.

After that, Akira and I never saw her in school again. We visited her house, but she refused to come out of her room to see us. Three months later, we learned that she was pregnant by a divorced Caucasian man. There was a rumor that he beat her.

As time went by, we learned that she was working at a restaurant. We went there, but she did not say much. We left the restaurant after leaving her a hefty tip. Eventually, Emi returned to Japan with her baby. I felt somewhat responsible for her fate.

After Emi and Akira returned to Japan, I was often alone, but I had other friends with whom I partied and hung around.

The Women's Libber

I met another student at Modesto Junior College named Cindy. She worked in the school cafeteria busing tables. Although she was not the best-looking girl in the school, I was still attracted to her. I wanted to show I was interested in her, so I started talking to her while she worked. Finally, I asked her out, and she agreed to go out with me.

She invited me to the house where she rented a room. While we were there, she confessed that she was a women's libber and asked if that intimidated me. I told her that it did not, as my father was not a typical, chauvinistic Japanese man, and neither was I. I passed the test. She asked me to spend the night with her, in her room, in a separate bed. By making the first move, I think she wanted to demonstrate that she was aggressive. I was not accustomed to forceful women then, and I spent the remainder of the evening acting like a wimpy dog waiting to be mauled by an aggressive bitch. Unfortunately, morning came, and nothing happened.

A few days later, I visited Cindy while her younger brother was with her. I was sitting at the piano fiddling around when Cindy unexpectedly and forcefully grabbed ahold of my arm and dragged me into her bedroom. It happened so quickly that I could not react. Next, she threw me on her bed like I was just a ragdoll and proceeded to maul me. Her brother saw what she did and stood at her bedroom door, knocking and pretending that he had something he wanted to talk to her about. That did not deter Cindy, as she continued to manhandle me physically. When it was all over, she emerged from the bedroom with a happy and satisfied look on her face.

I think she acted this way because she was frustrated that I was not sexually aggressive enough for her. She wanted to prove to me that she was a women's libber. Cindy constantly advocated for women's rights. She and her friends often designated certain dates to go around braless or without panties. This did not bother me at all. It meant I had fewer things to remove to get where I wanted to be.

Cindy the Streaker

Long before she met me, Cindy was known to go streaking with her friends. Whether they were male or female, she did it anyway. Fortunately, she had not been arrested.

One day, she asked me to go streaking with her and her friends past a public pool nearby. I politely declined her invitation for two reasons: little Mickey was not exactly a prize-winning item to show off in public, and I did not want to get arrested and deported to Japan.

Close Encounter with the Law

Cindy and I were driving in the Modesto countryside in my 1966 Mustang when I spotted a nice, fenced area for us to walk around. We crawled under the barbed wire fence and enjoyed the early summer scene. As we were walking, Cindy stopped and turned around, gazing at me with a certain look in her eyes. I had seen that look before and knew exactly what it meant.

I looked around for an area where I could meet my wild mare's needs, but we were in rough terrain with rocks all around. I finally found a large enough rock to accommodate us and quickly got to work with nature as our spectator. When we were finished, we walked back to my car. Just as we reached the Mustang, a police squad car pulled up. The officer asked us to sit on the ground and informed us that we were on private land. We had naively assumed that we were only being watched by nature, but it soon became apparent that the officer had also watched us.

Cindy was obviously shaken up. I was sure that the officer was going to give us a pink ticket and tell us to show up in court. Unlike my earlier petty theft incident, I did not see the policeman's gun; therefore, I did not imagine harming myself with it.

Over the next ten minutes, he copied down our drivers' license numbers and gathered additional information from us. We were relieved that he let us both go. After dating for three to four months, Cindy and I broke up.

Replacing One Horse with Another

After I sold my 1966 Mustang, I upgraded to a 1968 brown metallic Mustang fastback with a white interior. I purchased the car from a private seller and naively drove it only a few blocks, never exceeding twenty-five miles per hour. It was a beautiful car, and I fell in love with it. I paid the seller $500 and happily drove away in my newly purchased Mustang.

The next day, I took my new car on the freeway and heard loud knocking noises coming from under the hood. I was baffled. Afterward, when I checked under the hood, I realized that the big block engine was not bolted to the engine mounts and was just sitting on top of the inner fenders. It was like an overweight auntie getting her big derriere stuck in a small dining room arm chair. When I drove over forty miles per hour, the knocking sounds were louder. The knocking sounds were truly earsplitting when I drove the car on the freeway at eighty miles per hour. I could not stand it and stuffed cigarette butts in my ears until I got home.

I decided to go to Reno for a gambling excursion in the middle of winter, accompanied by three friends. We spent over six hours at the casinos and agreed to start our journey home in the morning. As morning came, we were all exhausted and sleepy. When we reached the top of the mountain on the freeway, we were stopped by the police and ordered to purchase snow chains before we would be allowed to proceed further. I purchased the snow chains, but they were too big for my tires. As soon as I started driving again, I could hear loud sounds coming from the back of my car as the oversized chains hit against the rear fenders. There was nothing I could do, so I continued driving that way for another hour and covered a distance of twenty miles. My passengers were so tired that they slept soundly for the duration of the trip, despite the deafening sounds of the chains striking the fenders. Again, I resorted to stuffing cigarette butts in my ears to help muffle the sound as I drove home.

I was mortified by the thought of the damage the chains were causing. Luckily, the chains did not damage the car.

Gambling Fever Strikes Again

What started as pachinko fever during my college years in Japan grew into something much worse in the U.S. When I lived in Stockton, my friend Kei and I regularly drove to Lake Tahoe, where I made some money playing blackjack. I believe this is what ignited my gambling addiction.

I had $500 each month to pay for rent, food, and gasoline. At that time, gasoline cost thirty-five cents a gallon. During summer vacation, I worked at various canneries to earn extra money. Unfortunately, any money that was left over went directly into gambling in Reno and Lake Tahoe.

Coasting on Fumes

Initially, when I was overcome with gambling fever, I gambled primarily in Lake Tahoe. In those days, one dollar blackjack tables were common. One day, I made up my mind to go to Lake Tahoe with $50 and some change in my pocket. I had a full tank of gas, but I knew that a full tank would not get me to Lake Tahoe and back.

About thirty miles into my trip, I was stopped for speeding. I attempted to bribe the police officer with $20, but it did not work. Still, a speeding ticket would never deter a gambling addict. I arrived in Lake Tahoe and in one hour I managed to lose the entire $50 at the blackjack table. Fortunately, I still had two one-dollar bills in my pocket. I quickly calculated that based on what I already had in the tank, if I added an additional $2 worth of gasoline, I would somehow make it back home. This is a typical gambler's mentality.

I put two dollars' worth of gas into the tank and started the drive back home. But I wanted some assurance that I could get home without running out of gas. Once I reached the highest point on the mountain, I turned off the engine and let the car coast down the freeway at a speed of about sixty miles per hour without power steering or brakes. It was a scary experience, but I did not have a choice.

As I was on the freeway, passing by Stockton, I thought about visiting Mark and borrowing some money from him for gas, even though Modesto was only twenty-five miles away. I decided to continue driving down the freeway and managed to get home with barely any gas left in the tank. Had I not coasted down the mountain, I probably would not have made it home. I was literally driving on fumes.

After this, I drove to Lake Tahoe or Reno quite often and lost every penny I brought with me.

Neither Snow nor Sleet nor Hail Shall Prevent a Gambler from Gambling

Toward the end of December 1973, I decided to go to Lake Tahoe. I arrived at four in the afternoon and went straight to the blackjack table. My luck that day was up and down, but after eight hours of gambling I lost the $100 I had brought with me. I was not worried about losing everything this time because when I arrived, I filled the gas tank in the car. I was sure that I would not have any trouble getting home.

When I left the casino, the temperature outside was hovering at zero degrees Fahrenheit. It took me almost ten minutes to locate my Mustang in the vast parking lot. I got into my car and turned the ignition key.

Nothing. The car engine would not crank. I checked the water in the radiator and saw that it was frozen, as it did not have any anti-freeze mixed in it. I was totally devastated.

I had one thin blanket and decided to sleep in the car that night while waiting for the bank to open the next morning. It was a horrendous night, and I thought I would freeze to death. It was extremely cold in the car, and my legs began feeling numb. I had poor blood circulation from sitting in the car all night.

I survived until morning, then I walked one mile on a slippery, snow-covered road to a Bank of America branch, where I withdrew $100. I walked back to my car and called for a tow truck. My car was towed to a nearby gas station. The mechanic told me that the freeze plugs in the engine block were ruptured. He could not repair them until the following week.

I paid the tow truck driver $10 and still had $90 in my pocket. My gambling-addicted brain told me that I could go back to the blackjack table and earn back the money I had lost earlier, plus I could win more money to pay for the car repair and the bus ticket back to Modesto. As you might expect, I lost everything except $10 in one hour.

I walked one mile to the Greyhound bus terminal and purchased a ticket to Modesto for $9. The bus bound for Modesto would not leave for another six hours, and I had not eaten for at least 24 hours. I spent the remaining $1 on snacks from a vending machine.

After a five-hour bus ride, I arrived at the Modesto Greyhound bus terminal. I tried calling a few friends to see if any of them would give me a ride back home, but it was Christmas. No one was home. I walked three miles from the bus terminal to my house.

The following week, I asked a friend to drive me to Lake Tahoe to pick up my car. After paying the mechanic for the repair, my friend and I went to the casino to play blackjack, only to lose more money.

I never learned my lesson and continued to do stupid things while gambling for the duration of my stay in Modesto.

A Gambler's Revenge

I asked a Japanese lady friend (not my girlfriend) to accompany me on a 200-mile trip to Reno. Before we left, she told me that if I lost all my money, we would come right back home. She made it clear that she would not lend me any money. I brought $100 with me, and as usual, I lost it all at the blackjack table. To my dismay, she kept her word. Even though I begged her numerous times, she refused to lend me any money.

We returned home, but I woke up the next morning with a strong desire to go back to Reno. I was pretty irritated at myself for losing $100. I withdrew another $100 from the bank and drove back to Reno.

When I arrived in Reno, I performed my usual ritual and filled my gas tank. I returned to the blackjack table, and in one hour, I lost $90. I returned home even more irritated than before.

The following morning, I woke up and went to the bank to withdraw another $100. I drove to Reno, and just like the previous day, I lost $90 at the blackjack table in one hour. After three days, I had driven 1,200 miles back and forth between Modesto and Reno, lost fifteen hours of my life, and was nearly $300 poorer.

Where Is My Car?

A month after the last incident, I decided to return to Reno for yet another revenge match. As usual, I filled up the gas tank after I arrived and went straight to the blackjack table.

After playing for four hours, I was down to my last $20. But to my surprise, my luck changed. I started winning. Within five hours or so, I had accumulated chips totaling $870. The casino pit boss approached me and offered me a room at his hotel, but I declined. Being a typical gambling addict, I wanted to keep on playing.

I continued to play blackjack through the night, and after about seventeen hours, I lost everything. During the entire time I was playing, I did not sleep or eat. I walked out of the casino and went to the spot where I thought I had parked my car, but it was nowhere to be found. I thought my mind was playing tricks on me due to my lack of sleep. I asked around and learned that my car was towed away for being illegally parked.

The towing company was located two miles away. I had no choice and went there on foot to find out how much I owed to get my car back. When I arrived, I learned that I had to pay $13.50. Since it was Saturday, no banks were open. I walked back to the casino and searched for nearby pawn shops. As a last resort, I was going to pawn my gold Tissot watch, which I had purchased at a duty-free shop in France for $70 back in 1971.

No pawn shops were open, so I asked people in the street if they would be interested in buying my watch. I finally found someone who was willing to pay $15 for my $70 Tissot. Once I had the money in my hands, my gambler's brain began to reason that I owed the towing company $13.50. I was certain that I had a couple of quarters in the glove compartment. So, I had a few dollars to return to the blackjack table to win back the money I had lost.

Not surprisingly, I lost the money two minutes after sitting at the table. As I was walking back to the towing company, I was praying very hard that there would be at least two quarters in the glove compartment to give me the $13.50 I needed to get my car back. Luckily, I found three quarters, which gave me more than I needed.

By this time, it had been twenty-four hours since I slept or had anything to eat. I had driven on the freeway for one hour when I realized I could no longer combat my exhaustion. I pulled over onto the shoulder and slept for two hours. I was fortunate that a highway patrolman did not find me. When I returned to Modesto, I had not slept or eaten for over thirty hours. My gambling addiction was completely out of control.

Pushing my Motorcycle

I wanted to visit a friend in Stockton, but rather than taking my car, I decided to ride my Yamaha motorcycle. I thought I had enough gas in the tank for the round trip, but I was mistaken.

About fifteen miles into my return trip on the freeway, my motorcycle was out of gas. I was forced to push it along the side of the freeway for ten miles in the middle of the night. This was extremely challenging as the side of the freeway was covered in gravel.

Weekend Nightlife

In 1973, I frequented a particular nightclub every Saturday night for five months. The club served alcohol and had a nice dance floor accommodating approximately fifty dancers. I usually went alone, but occasionally I met up with my female friends at the club. I went there with one purpose in mind, to pick up chicks.

Although I did not drink alcohol, I ordered a Bloody Mary and pretended to nurse it all night. I was not a very good dancer. In fact, people later told me that I danced like an out-of-control octopus. Imagine for a minute a young Japanese man dressed in a psychedelic shirt, a tight pair of purple pants, and brown shoes that did not match the outfit dancing like an out-of-control octopus. It is no wonder that only half of the girls I asked to dance accepted my invitation.

I stood with my back up against the wall while I surveyed the entire dance floor in search of my prey. When my favorite songs came on, I charged in for the kill.

Without exception, the evening always ended with the same slow song. As soon as we men heard the song, we frantically went in search of a dance partner. Finding a partner for the last dance often decided whether or not we could pick up a chick.

I had some tried-and-true methods for arousing my partner, which included whispering in her ear in my best Elvis Presley voice, "What are you planning to do after this?" Sometimes I succeeded, and other times, not so much.

The New 1968 Javelin

Eventually, I grew tired of my loud 1968 Mustang fastback and sold it. In its place, I purchased a 1968 AMC Javelin. It had some damage on the passenger side door, which I had fixed at the body shop. Later, I prepped the car for paint, took it to the same body shop, and had it painted bright red. Using a can of spray paint, I painted giant, white, wedge-like stripes on each side of the car, like the ones on the iconic Ford Gran Torino driven by Starsky and Hutch on the popular TV show.

In Modesto, every Saturday night was cruise night on McHenry Avenue. My car was so flashy that everyone liked it, particularly the girls. After just a few months of ownership, I sold the Javelin and bought a 1968 AMC AMX, for which I paid $925. The AMX was a two-seater that resembled a chopped-off Javelin with a much shorter wheel base. It was black with two white stripes painted on the hood, and I really liked viewing the body lines of that car from the side.

California Polytechnic State University (Cal Poly)

Modesto Junior College hosted a lot of college recruiters in the fall of 1974. I only spoke to the representative from Cal Poly in San Luis Obispo. I wanted to go to that school as the girl I had met in Stockton went there six months earlier. I also wanted to go somewhere far away from Lake Tahoe and Reno.

I explained to the college representative that I was a foreign student from Japan, and I only had a 3.2 grade point average. He assured me he would accept me after I submitted the required application. A few weeks later, I submitted my application and was accepted for the 1975 spring quarter. I was very fortunate to be accepted with a 3.2 GPA. Cal Poly is the most selective school in the California State University system. It accepted less than thirty percent of first year applicants, and the grade point average for the mid-50 percent of enrolled Cal Poly freshman is 4.08 to 4.25. I suppose I might have been accepted since I was a foreign student.

xiii. Circa 1977

San Luis Obispo

March 1975 – June 1977

Cal Poly

California Polytechnic State University in San Luis Obispo (Cal Poly SLO) has a sister school in Pomona, California known as California State Polytechnic University Pomona (Cal Poly Pomona). Since 1949, the two schools have jointly entered a float in the annual Pasadena Tournament of Roses Parade. The students design and build the floats themselves. Over the years, they have introduced several technologies into float building such as the use of hydraulics for animation and computer-controlled animation. They even grow their own flowers to decorate the floats. The student-built floats have won sixty awards over the years, including the Extraordinaire Trophy in 2023.

Life in San Luis Obispo

In March 1975, I packed my AMX with everything I owned and departed for San Luis Obispo. As I drove through the town to get to my dormitory, the scenery I encountered led me to believe that it was even more rural than Modesto. I was rather depressed for the next several months until I became more familiar with the area.

I secured a room at one of the on-campus dormitories known as Sequoia. I was informed beforehand that I would be sharing the room with another student. I was hoping I would be sharing the room with an American student, but he turned out to be a Japanese American instead. He was a pretty bright individual majoring in architecture. He had a car he was extremely proud of. It was a 1957 Chevy Bel Air two-door sedan. I did not care for the car and could not understand why it appealed to him so much. We never fought, but we were truly like the odd couple, Felix and Oscar.

Three hundred dollars per month paid for the dorm room and two meals per day at the school cafeteria. I paid $550 per quarter for my out-of-state tuition and $30 for my books. In addition to the tuition money, my parents still sent me $1,500 every three months.

I was accepted into Cal Poly as a junior. The 90 credit units I had earned at Tokyo International University in Japan went toward meeting the requirements for a Bachelor of Science degree in Business Administration with a focus on management. Except for the summer quarter, I attended every quarter as a full-time student until I graduated in June 1977.

Cal Poly was located near the towns of Avila Beach and Pismo Beach. When the weather got warm, we went to the beaches to relax. On weekends, we cruised right on Pismo Beach. There was a long, wide stretch of sand to drive on; we did not need a four-wheel drive vehicle.

Brian and Gary

I befriended two American students at the school cafeteria. Their names were Brian and Gary, and they shared a dormitory room. Of the two of them, Brian was particularly friendly toward me. One day, I visited their dorm room. As Brian and I were talking, Gary flew into a jealous rage. He started crying and throwing books at Brian. I did not understand what was happening, so I left.

About an hour later, there was a knock on my door. When I opened it, I saw Gary standing there looking rather downtrodden. I let him in my room, and he started to explain the situation with tears welling up in his eyes. Gary said he grew jealous of me because Brian was paying attention to me. He apologized several times while gazing intently into my eyes. This made me feel very uncomfortable, even though he stood three feet away from me.

I had never encountered such a situation before and did not know how to react. I could not even anticipate what Gary was going to do next. In the end, I accepted his apology, and he left.

The Professional Dancer

Gary revealed he had been a professional dancer, and told me the story of how he was once arrested for indecent exposure. He had been hitchhiking and was picked up by a trucker driving a canvas-back truck. He climbed into the back, and they proceeded onto the freeway. On the freeway, Gary noticed a car following them. He had an idea to show off his dancing skills to the passengers in that car.

He changed into his birthday suit, flipped up the canvas cover, and began to dance while focusing on moving his rather over-sized manhood in every direction possible. This escapade led to his arrest, and subsequently he was thrown into jail.

Pirates Cove Nude Beach

After Gary's jealous rage, the three of us became good friends. One day, they invited me to visit a public nude beach with them. I initially declined, explaining that I had never been to a nude beach. They assured me that I did not need to remove my clothes, and I would enjoy the scenery. They also gave me a tip about placing a strip of photo negative film over my eyes so the girls would not know what I was looking at.

So, off we went. When we arrived, we found a place behind a big rock. Approximately ten feet in front of us were three young girls, possibly Cal Poly students, who were sunning themselves. Brian and Gary completely disrobed while I kept my jeans and shirt on. Brian was sitting, leaning against the rock, but Gary promptly positioned himself in front of the rock. He proceeded to pose like a model with a huge grin on his face. He looked down at the three girls, hoping they would notice him.

A little later, one of the girls caught a glimpse of Gary's "pride" and gestured to the others to look at him. All three had shocked looks on their faces. After getting the recognition he craved, Gary flashed a big smile. His mission was accomplished. This was the first and the last time I visited a nude beach.

Living with Brian and Gary for a Month

After living in the school dorm for just one quarter, I decided to move out. I moved in with Brian and Gary, who rented a one-bedroom apartment. They slept on a queen bed in the bedroom while I slept on a twin mattress on the living room floor. We were going about our lives and doing our own things.

One day, Brian sat me down and said, "Mickey, I know you like girls." Then he proceeded to elucidate the benefits of sleeping with another man. I was rather shocked by his comments and did not respond. Aside from this incident, I enjoyed their company.

New Apartment

After I parted ways with Brian and Gary, I moved into a three-bedroom apartment with David and Richard. David and I did a lot of things together, but I avoided Richard, who seemed a little odd to me.

The school was only a quarter of a mile away from my new apartment, but I drove my car to school every day. I suppose I was just too lazy to walk. This was when I learned how to do bodywork on cars. I caused an accident that damaged the left front fender of my AMX. I used the apartment's parking lot to repair my car. I removed the fender, repaired the damage with Bondo body filler, and painted it with several cans of black spray paint. I liked the end result.

Later on, I heard that Brian and Gary quit school.

The School Auto Hobby Club

There was an auto hobby club at Cal Poly. It had a small garage on campus equipped with a compressor and a spray gun. This is where I began to perfect my autobody repair skills.

I prepped my AMX using various grades of sandpaper and completely masked it with newspapers. Using the compressor and spray gun, I painted it bright red, just like my 1968 AMC Javelin. The paint job came out flawlessly, and I was quite happy with my work.

I purchased a pair of used wheels with big tires and rear air shocks. I filled the air shocks to the maximum capacity to alter the car's stance. From the side, it looked like a sprinter getting ready to start. This was the beginning of my love affair with car bodywork and modifications.

Humiliating Race

One day, I was bragging to a friend about how fast my AMX could run. He became annoyed with me and challenged me to a race against his 1971 Chevy Camaro SS with its big block 396 engine. I boldly accepted his challenge.

On the day of the race, he arrived with his girlfriend sitting in the passenger side of his Camaro. We lined up our cars in front of a traffic signal. When the light changed from red to green, I floored the accelerator. Unfortunately, my AMX was no match for his souped-up engine. I was humiliated beyond words. To cover my embarrassment, I used the excuse that the huge tires I had installed in the back of my car caused me to accelerate at a much slower rate.

Not a Model Student

I was not exactly a model student. As long as I maintained a 3.0 grade point average, I was happy. Unless submitting homework was required, I did not do any. Unless taking notes in class was absolutely necessary, I did not take notes in class. I only opened the textbook the night before an exam and read the pages pertaining to the test. I did this for the majority of my classes and earned B grades. I was not a genius by any means, but I had an incredible memory.

The only classes for which I received a D were American Government and Biology 101. I attended a few Biology 101 classes, but I soon got bored as a great deal of the material included in this class was already covered in my high school classes in Japan. I stopped going to class, except on the days when the midterm and final exams were given.

Although I never submitted the weekly homework, I still received an honorable D, a passing grade, for my minimal effort.

As for the American Government class, my test preparation method was ineffective due to the enormous number of pages I needed to read. Also, one-third of the questions on the test came from lectures. In hindsight, I should have designated these classes "for credit only" rather than risk low grades impacting my GPA.

Playing the Losing Game

I moved further away from the casinos I used to frequent, but I could not move away from my gambling habit.

Before the spring quarter of 1975 came to an end, I made up my mind to move out of the three-bedroom apartment. I arranged to share an apartment with another male student at Cal Poly during the summer months. A week before I was to move in with him, I packed up all of my belongings, put them in my AMX, and drove almost 500 miles to Las Vegas to have some fun.

However, my fun turned into disaster after I lost the money that would have gone toward paying the rent and other expenses for the summer. When I returned to San Luis Obispo, I informed the student that I could not move in with him. Rather than tell him the truth, I made up some excuse. Understandably, he was extremely upset. I only had $100 in my pocket and did not want to ask my parents for more money.

Then, while working on my car, a small metal piece got imbedded in my right eye. I did not have enough money to go to a doctor. Instead, I drove to a nearby Taco Bell, and in the parking lot I removed the metal piece from my eye using a needle from my sewing kit while looking into my rear-view mirror.

Fortunately, I found a room to rent for the summer costing only $50 a month. Through a friend, I found a job working in the mess hall at Camp San Luis Obispo. This was an Army reserve camp where the soldiers trained during the summer. My duties included serving breakfast and lunch, cleaning the metal serving trays, and doing general cleaning. I worked eight hours a day, from 6 a.m. until 2:30 p.m., for thirty days non-stop. I woke up at 5:30 a.m. every day to go to work. After one week, I woke up in the morning and noticed I had difficulty tying my shoelaces. It was due to overusing my hands and fingers.

On the last day, we worked almost 24 hours straight cleaning the entire mess hall until it was spotless. We even cleaned the ovens and the grill tops. We were allowed to rest for one hour on the concrete floor. The day also happened to be the Mexican sergeant's last day at Camp San Luis Obispo. When I saw him, I said, "Hey, sergeant! I am going to miss you so f'--- much that I could s---- in my pants!" I thought I sounded pretty damn American, but all of my coworkers, who were Cal Poly students, were shocked when they heard my comment. They later told me that they thought I was going to get punched, but being a foreigner saved me. In the end, I was happy that the sergeant was not angry with me. This job saved my summer.

New Place Until Graduation

To save money, at the end of the winter quarter in 1976, I moved into a rundown, old, one-bedroom apartment. The rent was $100 a month, and the old lady who owned the place walked to my apartment on the first day of each month to collect it.

My new place was located in the downtown area, about two miles from the campus. I still recall typing my 16-page graduation thesis on an IBM typewriter in this apartment. I wish that ChatGPT, the general-purpose chatbot that uses artificial intelligence to generate text, had been available to write my paper for me.

I lived in this apartment until I graduated from Cal Poly in June 1977.

The Girl with the Bluest Eyes

During the spring quarter of 1976, I enrolled in a class that was required for all seniors majoring in business administration. We were divided into five-person discussion groups. In my group was a girl with the bluest eyes I had ever seen. She was not the cutest girl in class, but I was drawn to her deep blue eyes. Her name was Madeline, and she had dark hair. I was not attracted to women with dark hair, but I wanted to get to know her better.

Unfortunately, my only opportunity to speak with her was during our discussion group. When the quarter ended, she returned to her home in Los Angeles for the summer. I thought about her blue eyes every day, and I finally decided to write her a love letter.

After I obtained her address from the Student Union, I searched through various magazines to find photos of blue-eyed models. I cut out the eyes from the magazine pages and pasted them all over my love letter, about ten sets of blue eyes in all. In my letter, I told her I had fallen in love with her blue eyes and wanted to take them out for dinner. I signed the letter, "Your secret admirer." In a matter of days, I received the response I was expecting. She wrote back, "How about the rest of me?"

When she returned to San Luis Obispo, curiosity forced her to drive by the return address I had provided in my letter. At that moment, I happened to be standing outside my apartment. Upon seeing me, she seemed happy to learn that it was me who had sent her the letter.

She invited me to her girls-only dorm room that weekend. I arrived at 8 p.m. Her room was more spacious than my old dorm room. It was furnished with two single beds placed next to the walls at the opposite ends of the room. We talked until midnight. When it was time for me to leave, she suggested I spend the night in her roommate's bed since it was getting late. I had heard that suggestion several times before. I now loved aggressive girls.

I did not want to miss this opportunity, so I accepted her invitation. At first, I acted like a gentleman and laid on her roommate's bed. After she turned off the light, I snuck over to the battleground, where the war began. I saw her a few more times, but eventually I stopped seeing her because I wasn't attracted to girls with dark hair.

Joni

I worked at the university's language lab during the fall quarter of 1976. My main duty was to hand out cassette tapes to students. One day, a female student walked over to my counter with a big smile. She was interested in tapes about the Japanese language. She asked me a few questions about the tapes then walked over to a booth, where she spent the next thirty minutes. While she was sitting in the booth, she kept glancing over at me as if she were flirting. It made me feel pretty uncomfortable. When she came back to the counter to return the tapes, we talked for a minute or so. Then she left.

On her third visit, she introduced herself and asked me a lot of personal questions. Her name was Joni. From then on, we started going out together. Aside from my charm, I think she was interested in me because I was Japanese. She fit the bill for me as well, since she was a Caucasian, in my age group, and interested in Japanese men. I started hanging around her tiny studio apartment all the time, although I still kept my own apartment.

Decision Time

As graduation approached, I decided to return to Japan and find a job. I enjoyed my time in America, but felt I needed to fulfil my obligation to my parents. After all, they financed my entire college education in Japan and the U.S. In fact, my mother told me that she and my father had spent over $100,000 in seven years for my schooling. Later, I borrowed another $100,000 from my parents to buy my first and second houses in the U.S., without any intention of paying them back. Admittedly, I was a money-sucking leech.

I received a letter from Proctor & Gamble in the spring of 1977 advising that they were interested in hiring me for their Osaka office. My relationship with Joni had become more serious, and even though I had not officially proposed to her, I asked her to accompany me to Japan to see if she could live there. She agreed, and I called my parents to let them know that Joni was coming with me to Japan. Of course, they did not like it; my mother had warned me about bringing an American girl back with me before I left. I purchased roundtrip tickets for Joni and me just in case Japan was not to my liking this time around. My parents were not aware that I intended to return to the U.S.

xiv. Graduation photo

Nagano Homecoming

July 1977 - October 1977

After graduating with a Bachelor of Science degree in June, I left for Japan on July 6 with Joni by my side. We arrived in Tokyo and went straight to my parents' house in Nagano. My mother was a patient person, and my father was very easy-going. They were not hostile toward Joni, but I had no idea if they liked her.

Before I arrived in Nagano, my parents had lined up a job for me, assisted by my cousin, who is six years older than I. As soon as I mentioned my potential job opportunity with Proctor & Gamble in Osaka, they grew upset with me. They were expecting me to remain in Nagano with them. Consequently, I gave up the idea of working for P&G.

I had three weeks before starting my new job and decided to give Joni a tour of Nagano. She seemed to enjoy it. My cousin knew a man who was married to an American woman. Since they were living nearby, he introduced them to us. I was happy that Joni met them and hoped she could envision a future life living in Japan with me.

New Job at a Medical Device Manufacturing Company

Despite other people's objections, the company vice president really liked me and hired me. Apparently, there had been an earlier incident in town where another company had hired an individual who had returned from the U.S. with a degree. Not long after being hired, that individual quit and returned to the U.S.

I was assigned to the planning department, but since the vice president wanted me to learn about their products first, I was sent to the production section. The company produced very sophisticated and expensive medical devices.

I was always mechanically oriented and good with my hands, so I really liked my new job. However, I was very frustrated with the way they manufactured their devices; they used very antiquated methods. I wanted to shorten the production time and came up with a few tools that accomplished that goal. A lot of people in the organization liked my ideas and were very supportive of me. I thought I had a bright future with this company.

At the time, the youngest employee promoted to senior manager was 32 years old. I was eager and wanted to be promoted to a managerial position at a much younger age.

Pachinko Fever Returns

While I enjoyed my new job, Joni was alone at my parents' house. Once in a while, my cousin's eight-year-old daughter visited her, but that wasn't enough to soothe her loneliness. At the time, I did not realize how lonely she felt.

It had been over eight years since I last played Pachinko, so I dropped by the Pachinko parlor after work a few times for 30 to 40 minutes without telling Joni first. I believe she knew what I was doing when I came home late.

One evening, when I returned home late after playing Pachinko, my mother told me she had not seen Joni for a while. I was worried about her, so I went out looking for her on my bicycle. I finally reached the riverbank and saw a petite figure sitting on the edge of the river about a quarter of a mile away.

As I approached closer, I recognized that it was Joni. She looked very despondent, and she was not happy with me. Even though she did not say much, I believe she had made up her mind; this was not the kind of life she wanted to spend with me in Japan.

Ten days after this incident, I said good-bye to her at Haneda Airport in Tokyo.

A Life-Changing Moment

After Joni returned to the U.S., I wrote to her every other day. The first letter I received back from her was devastating. She stated that things would not work out for us in Japan and we should go our separate ways. As soon as I read her letter, my brain went blank. I panicked.

That night, I had a huge fight with my parents. I told them I was leaving for the U.S. the next day to see Joni. They knew my mind was made up.

It was very distressing for my parents to learn that I was leaving them again. They had waited over seven years for me, their only son, to return to Nagano to live with them. Now I planned to leave again, and they did not know if I would ever come back. Around that time, in rural Japan, the oldest son or the eldest child would live with their parents and take care of them.

I agonized over what I was about to do. That night, I wrote a lengthy letter to my parents with tears welling up in my eyes. I apologized to them and expressed my determination. I was packed and ready to leave in the morning. I took a taxi to the train station, where my father met me a little later. He gave me $500 and suggested that I speak with the company vice president. I thought it was the right thing to do, since he had gone against the advice of others to hire me.

He was surprised to learn that I was leaving for the U.S. I deeply apologized for my behavior and left. I stayed overnight at my high school friend's house in Tokyo and departed Japan on October 1, 1977.

xv. With my parents, circa 1977

Back in the U.S.A.

In Trouble in Hawaii

My flight back to the U.S. included a connecting flight that landed in Honolulu before proceeding to the mainland. Ever since I had received that letter from Joni, my mind had been acting crazy. I was unable to think logically.

I stepped up to the immigration counter in Honolulu and went through the standard questioning process with the immigration officer. When he asked me what the purpose of my trip was and how long I planned to stay in the U.S., I blurted out, "I came here to get married to my girlfriend in California, and after that I am planning to get a green card." My reply might have been the worst response to give to an immigration officer. It set off all kinds of bells and alarms. He calmly asked me to step over to a different counter.

The officer at the second counter asked me if I had a return ticket to Japan. At this point, I realized that I was in big trouble. I might even be denied entry into the U.S. and told to go back to Japan. I explained that I did not have a return ticket, but I had the money to purchase one. In desperation, I showed him the letter I had received from Joni, and I told him that I really needed to speak with her.

Since Joni did not have a telephone in her apartment, they could not call her to verify my statement. As time passed, I grew more despondent and began to cry and begged them to give me one week to speak to her. Luckily, the officer had a soft spot for love and romance. After thirty minutes of pleading with him, he allowed me to stay in the United States for two weeks. He let me go with a final warning. "Make sure to return to Japan in two weeks!"

They say everything happens for a reason. The compassion the immigration officer showed me that day changed my life forever.

Waiting in Los Angeles

After my flight landed at Los Angeles International Airport, I checked into a nearby hotel on Century Boulevard. I called a friend in San Luis Obispo and asked him to get in touch with Joni and ask her to come and pick me up at the hotel. Los Angeles was a two-hundred-mile trip from San Luis Obispo, and she did not have a car. My friend called back and told me they were on their way.

While I waited, it felt as though I was suffocating inside my hotel room. I went outside in the dark and nervously paced back and forth on Century Boulevard, like a caged tiger. It was probably a bad idea to walk up and down that street late at night. I could have easily been robbed or assaulted. I was completely out of mind. Joni and my friend arrived after midnight.

Back in San Luis Obispo

I don't recall the conversations that Joni and I had in the car on the drive back to San Luis Obispo. We arrived at her apartment around 4:30 in the morning and went to bed. After that, we acted like nothing had happened. We continued living like we did before we went to Japan together.

However, after one week of living together, someone knocked on her door. When I opened the door, I saw a young Japanese American guy standing there who wanted to speak to Joni. I thought it was rather strange for her to have visitors, since she did not have any visitors to her apartment when we were together prior to leaving for Japan. Joni hurriedly came to the door while I retreated back into the room. She started speaking to the guy in a deliberately audible voice. I heard her tell him, "My boyfriend came back from Japan…"

I soon realized what was happening. Joni came back from Japan in a very depressed state and found another guy right away. I did not ask her who he was and pretended it did not bother me. However, after that incident my relationship with Joni changed.

While I was there, my friend was kind enough to let me borrow his 1972 yellow Datsun pickup truck. The clutch was slipping, so I replaced the clutch and pressure plate and got it running perfectly.

After another three weeks passed, I finally decided to move on and left Joni for good.

My Life as an Illegal Alien

Since I did not return to Japan in two weeks, as I had promised the immigration officer, I was officially considered an illegal alien. I still had $300 and many Japanese friends who were students at Cuesta Community College in San Luis Obispo. I had met many of them before I returned to Japan, and some of these friends knew Joni. They were all at least five years younger than I, and they addressed me as Mickey-san. In Japan, it is customary to address older or more prominent people with the honorific "san." If the individual is younger, we use "kun" after their first or last name.

I was fortunate that many of them allowed me to stay in their apartments for weeks at a time. Without their help, I probably would not be writing this book. I appreciate each and every one of them for helping me in my time of need. Most of these friends returned to Japan by 1983.

Suzuki-kun

He arrived in San Luis Obispo in late 1976 to attend Cuesta College. His family was well off, and Suzuki-kun was a nice, kind-hearted person. However, his actions were nothing short of amazing when it came to cars.

Before arriving in California, he drove his Lotus Elite on a Tokyo freeway. Somehow, he managed to total that car. In the three years he lived in San Luis Obispo, he went through cars faster than a kid chasing after an ice cream truck. The first car he purchased in the U.S. was a used 1971 Camaro SS 396. That was the car I competed against in a race with my AMX and lost miserably. Next, he bought a used 1973 Triumph TR6, followed by a new 1978 Pontiac Trans Am.

One rainy day, Suzuki-kun and his girlfriend, Michiko, were on their way to my apartment. He took the Trans Am around a narrow curve at a high rate of speed, lost control of the car, and crashed into a tree. Luckily, they were both safe, but the car sustained substantial damage. After this, he purchased a used 1976 Corvette Stingray.

Upon returning to Japan, Michiko became a professional dancer and continued dancing until she was 39 years old. She was one of the prominent television background dancers for famous singers. While other dancers made $30 per appearance, she earned $500.

One day, Suzuki-kun was driving with Michiko again. They were on their way to Avila Beach, and he once again took a curve too fast and slid into a grassy ditch. Unlike the Trans Am, the Corvette was totaled. I purchased that car from him just before he returned to Japan, and I later traded it for a 1965 Corvette. But Suzuki-kun's traffic troubles did not end there.

We were having a party at his rented house in Morro Bay one night, and there was a knock on the door. When we opened the front door, there were two cops who had an arrest warrant for Suzuki-kun. Apparently, he had many outstanding traffic infractions and they took him to the county jail.

The banks were closed, and we needed money to bail him out. We forcefully convinced Tanimoto-kun, the youngest among us, to surrender the title of his 1976 Triumph Spitfire to the bail bondsman. We managed to get Suzuki-kun out of jail at three o'clock the next morning. He was to make a court appearance in two weeks.

When his court date came, I accompanied him to the Santa Maria Municipal Court. Before he appeared in front of the judge, I told him I would act as his advisor and take care of him. When Suzuki-kun was called, I accompanied him and pretended to be his translator. I translated what the judge said, but I told Suzuki-kun to say whatever he wanted to me, and I turned around and told the judge what I thought he wanted to hear. This went on for a while. At some point, the judge stopped and asked me if I was really translating what he said to the defendant. Of course, I replied with a firm, "Yes, sir!"

When it was all said and done, Suzuki-kun was placed on probation for two years. He ultimately served just one year and returned to Japan in 1979.

Suzuki-kun was very well-mannered and knew the fine points of *omotenashi* (Japanese hospitality). Whenever we visited his apartment, which he shared with Michiko, he always handed us a bong (water pipe) and a lighter as though he was serving us a cup of tea or coffee. It was how he made his guests feel welcome in his home. Within our SLO circle, we never called marijuana "pot." Among us, it was always "mezzo," something Suzuki-kun had actually started.

Later, Suzuki-kun succeeded his father's business in Japan, and he became a successful business man. He has lived in Japan for forty years now and has married four times. His current wife is twenty-one years his junior. He continues to be a car connoisseur. He currently owns four very expensive cars.

Endo-kun

Endo-kun was Suzuki-kun's former high school classmate, and he arrived in San Luis Obispo in 1977. Like Suzuki-kun, he was a car connoisseur but a much better driver. During his three-year stay in SLO, he owned a 1975 yellow Camaro, a 1968 flared Volkswagen Bug, and a 1978 Datsun 280Z. His favorite activities were reading manga and playing *Space Invaders* at the pizza parlor.

After attending Cuesta College, he returned to Japan in January 1980. A short while later, he married his first wife. Endo-kun returned to San Luis Obispo unexpectedly in 1986 and was rather conflicted. He had been seeing another woman, who eventually became his second wife. He was unsure whether he should file for a divorce from his wife.

I suggested we use a deck of cards to help him decide whether he should file for divorce. We played three games, and each time the result favored him filing for divorce.

Within a few days, Endo-kun returned to Japan and filed for a divorce from his first wife. A few months later, he arrived in San Luis Obispo and started to live with one of our mutual friends. He later became my roommate when I moved down to Los Angeles.

Saito-kun

Saito-kun joined us in SLO in March 1978. He was a student at Cuesta College, and just as much of a car destroyer as Suzuki-kun. Among the cars he annihilated were a 1983 Dodge Charger, a 1975 Honda Civic, and a 1971 Ford Capri. The only car he did not demolish was a yellow 1965 Corvette he purchased from me.

He returned to Japan in October 1983, and he was to sell the 1965 Corvette back to me on the day of his departure. However, based on what a mutual friend told me, Saito-kun drove the car hard along the winding mountain roads before turning it over to me. I suppose he wanted to enjoy the car one last time. The day after he departed for Japan, the water pump started leaking.

Saito-kun was not only hard on his own vehicles. He also abused cars that did not belong to him. Takada-kun (I will discuss him a little later) returned to Japan during the summer break and asked Saito-kun to take care of his 1973 Charger while he was away. One night, when it was pitch-dark outside, Saito-kun took the car on an unpaved, winding mountain road. He must have been speeding and did not realize that the road ahead of him was about to end. The Charger went over the edge of a 100-foot cliff with Saito-kun inside. Saito-kun was unconscious when two ladies found him.

When he regained consciousness, he found himself in a hospital bed. Fortunately, his injuries were not severe or life-threatening. This incident did little to change Saito-kun's driving habits, however. He rolled a Honda Civic and crashed a Ford Capri.

Takada-kun

Like the others, Takada-kun came to SLO to attend Cuesta College. He arrived in September 1976 and returned to Osaka four years later. Eventually, he was joined by his older and younger brothers, who also became students at Cuesta.

Takada-kun was the son of an otolaryngologist, and his family was well off in Japan. He was a tall and very mellow individual. He had ambitions of becoming a professional bowler, so we went bowling together often.

As I wrote earlier, he owned the 1973 Dodge Charger that Saito-kun wrecked. During his stay in SLO, Takada-kun also owned a 1970 Datsun 510 with flared fenders and a new 1978 Volkswagen Scirocco.

Takada-kun and I became roommates in 1978 and shared a one-bedroom apartment near Cal Poly. Looking back, I have to say that I spent some of the best times in San Luis Obispo there.

Four years after returning to Japan, Takada-kun got married. He brought his new bride to SLO for their honeymoon. One of our friends reserved a nice room for them at the famous Madonna Inn. Established in 1958, Madonna Inn sits on over 1,000 acres just off Highway 101, just minutes from downtown San Luis Obispo. It is known for its individually-themed guest rooms and whimsical settings, including a pink dining room. In fact, the predominant color throughout the hotel is pink.

It had been four years since I last saw Takada-kun. I asked our friend who had reserved the room to let me borrow the room key. He obliged. I knew the approximate time Takada-kun and his bride were to arrive at Madonna Inn. Before their arrival, I let myself into their room, then I hid under the bedspread trying to make my body as flat as possible in an effort not to get noticed. I waited patiently for their arrival.

After ten minutes had passed, I heard the couple enter the room. They were too busy talking to each other and setting up their luggage to notice me. After a few minutes, I fiercely threw off the bedspread and jumped up screaming, "Waaa…!!!" in a loud voice. They were both shocked and surprised; his wife was surprised a little more than Takada-kun.

Takada-kun regained his composure after fifteen seconds and exclaimed, "Mickey-san! You scared the hell out of me!" His young bride still had not figured out what had just happened. Takada-kun finally introduced me to her as crazy Mickey-san.

Tanimoto-kun

When he arrived in 1978, Tanimoto-kun was the youngest among us and a student at Cuesta College. He was the one we convinced to surrender the title of his 1976 Triumph Spitfire to bail out Suzuki-kun. That was very painful as his car was everything to him. If he found a minor blemish on his car, he got depressed and confined himself to his room. The only way he could combat his depression was by pleasuring himself. I knew this because I caught him in the act twice when I entered his room unannounced.

After he returned to Japan in 1981, he established a very successful business with a partner, and he earned a substantial income from it. At the peak of his success, he built an in-home movie theater and purchased a very expensive and much sought-after Nissan GTR, which he kept secret from his wife. He parked the car in a nearby rented garage and walked there from his house whenever he felt the urge to drive it. When I visited Japan in 1990 with my daughters, Tanimoto-kun picked us up at our hotel and drove us around in his GTR. It was a beautiful, fast car.

Unfortunately, his business partner embezzled money from their business, which eventually went down the drain. His misery was compounded when his wife divorced him.

Yamada-kun

I had a habit of walking in on my friends during the most awkward moments. Yamada-kun was among my many victims.

One day, five Japanese friends and I gathered at the parking lot of the apartment I shared with Tanaka-kun to work on my car. Yamada-kun suddenly announced that he had to use the restroom and went into my apartment. A few minutes later, I found that I had to answer nature's call and headed toward the bathroom, completely forgetting that Yamada-kun had gone there before me.

I rushed upstairs and thought it was odd when I saw that the bathroom door was closed. Tanaka-kun and I usually left the bathroom door open. Not giving the matter a second thought, I threw the door open only to find Yamada-kun sitting there pleasuring himself. I could not believe my eyes. It was such a shocking image that it is still burned into my brain today.

I stood there silently as Yamada-kun proceeded with virtuosic proficiency, completely unaware that I was watching him. I moved my eyes from his hand to his face, and our eyes met. It was the most ineffably awkward moment for the two of us.

Yamada-kun seemed incensed that I had witnessed his scared ritual, but he could not stop what he was doing. We gazed at each other silently until Yamada-kun shattered the stillness with the words, "Mickey-san! What are you doing?" These words pulled me out of the trance I was in. I laughed, shut the door, and ran to the parking lot to tell everyone what I had just seen.

When Yamada-kun returned, I confronted him, but he repeatedly denied it in front of everybody. I stopped talking about it because I did not want to embarrass him any further.

Omura-kun

Omura-kun was in the same age group as the other students I described earlier. Our meeting was rather unusual, but Omura-kun was a little unusual.

The one-bedroom apartment I shared with Takada-kun eventually evolved into Delta House from the 1978 National Lampoon film *Animal House*. Our friends were allowed to hang out in the apartment regardless of whether or not Takada-kun and I were there.

One day, I came home after work and saw that some of my friends were already hanging out in the apartment, but there was one guy that I did not recognize. He introduced himself as Omura and was very talkative about his past.

He had just arrived from Connecticut after being expelled from the seventh high school. He said that he had been expelled from six different high schools in Japan. The story was easy to believe after I got to know him better. He was financially supported by his parents. They were not extremely well off, but they sent him as much money as he requested and whenever he wished.

I had to go to bed around ten, but my friends and Omura-kun were still there. I went to bed anyway, and when I woke up at six the next morning, I found Omura-kun sleeping on a chair with its back leaning against the wall. Surprised to see him there, I kicked the seat as hard as I could to wake him up. The kick jarred his body, and he moved forward, sitting straight up on the chair. Unaware of what had just happened, he said, "Good morning! Mickey-san, I fell asleep on the chair." Without saying a word, I left the apartment to go to work.

From that moment on, for a period of several months, Omura-kun stealthily found his way into our apartment. Some days, I woke up and found him sleeping on the floor or the couch. Other days, he was there when I returned from work. I resorted to unorthodox methods of waking him up. At times, I poured a bucket of water over his head. Other times, I rolled a newspaper page into a tube, set fire to it, then placed the burning paper under his nose.

Omura-kun was a heavy pot smoker and bought the best pot he could afford. He found a dealer in San Luis Obispo, and every time he bought the "good stuff," he showed off by saying, "Mickey-san, look at these beautiful buds and smell their sweet scent." I have to admit that I had never seen pot as good as what he purchased back then. I finally realized that he was spending far too much money on weed and not doing anything with his life. I spoke to his mother in Tokyo over the phone and offered to manage his money. She gladly accepted and sent money intended for Omura-kun to my bank account. I gave Omura-kun $50 a week for pot. It was substantially less than the $200 per week he was accustomed to spending. He begged me for more money, but I did not budge.

When Suzuki-kun and Takada-kun shared a house in Morro Bay, they allowed Omura-kun to stay there while they spent their summer vacation in Japan. Omura-kun did not have a car then, so he was isolated. I wanted to teach him a harsh life lesson, so I advised everyone not to visit him for three days. According to my friends, he had hardly any food in the house and very little money on him.

On the third day of being isolated, at 7 a.m., I found Omura-kun sitting at a table in the restaurant where I worked as a dishwasher. It was very odd. He told me he had walked all night from Morro Bay, which was ten miles away. He did so because he did not have any food or money. I told him I would talk to him later and went back to the kitchen. When I returned to the restaurant area five minutes later, Omura-kun was gone. He had left me a short note saying, "Mickey-san, thank you very much for all you have done for me, but I cannot take it anymore. I will never see you again." But I knew Omura-kun better than that. I later found him at a friend's apartment. After that, I was less severe as far as money was concerned.

I later learned from Suzuki-kun that an SLO bank had mistakenly deposited $10,000 into Omura-kun's account. As soon as Omura-kun discovered the money, he withdrew the entire amount and spent it. By the time the bank discovered its error, it was too late. Omura-kun told the bank he had already spent all the money and did not have the funds to pay it back. The bank eventually gave up and stopped pursuing him. About a year after the incident, Omura-kun returned to Japan.

When my wife and I visited Japan thirteen years ago, we met Omura-kun in Tokyo. He offered me a joint right there, out in the open. I was surprised to learn that he was still a heavy pot smoker. I politely declined his offer. In Japan, pot is considered a hard drug, along with heroin and cocaine. If an individual is caught with pot, they face jail time.

Sadly, Omura-kun passed away from esophageal cancer in April 2014. I have many fond memories of him and miss him very much.

Kuroda-kun

Unlike my other friends who came to San Luis Obispo to attend Cuesta College, Kuroda-kun attended my alma mater, Cal Poly. He did not graduate from Cal Poly and transferred to UC Berkeley instead.

One night around 10 p.m., someone knocked on the front door of my apartment. I opened the door, and Kuroda-kun stood there looking dejected and disturbed. I invited him in and listened to what he had to say. Kuroda-kun told me he was suffering from hemorrhoids and asked for my advice. I asked him how his hemorrhoids came about. He told me his American girlfriend had inserted a foreign object into his rectum during sex. I told him he had come to the right place because this was one area about which I was rather knowledgeable. I offered my advice, and he left.

Three days later, he showed up at my friend's apartment while we watched a Lakers' basketball game. Again, he appeared tormented by his hemorrhoids and asked me to examine him. Initially I refused, but I eventually gave in after he persistently asked me to do it.

My friend brought over a very bright flashlight, and we proceeded with the examination as Kuroda-kun lay on his side. As soon as we caught sight of the monstrous purple hemorrhoids, we burst into laughter. After our laughter subsided, I advised Kuroda-kun to continue following my initial advice. He has never brought up the subject again.

Never Laugh at Your Neighbor

What qualified me to give Kuroda-kun advice on his hemorrhoids? I had suffered from a bleeding variety for a long time. When I relocated to Los Angeles from San Luis Obispo in 1986, I had endured enough suffering and decided to have them surgically removed.

I decided to seek out a suitable gastroenterologist or a proctologist. Anyone who has had a rectal examination for cancer or hemorrhoids knows that the process can be quite uncomfortable, and even painful at times. Therefore, it is imperative for the doctor conducting the examination to have small fingers. When I called various doctor's offices, I asked the receptionist if she would please go and check whether the doctor had big fingers.

Finally, I found Dr. McGarvey. His staff assured me that he had slender fingers. Yet, when I saw him for the first time, I asked him to show me his fingers just to be absolutely sure that the staff was telling me the truth. Fortunately for me, the doctor passed my visual inspection.

The doctor was a nice fellow, and he explained the procedure to me in detail. We set the surgery date for one week after my office visit. One day before the surgery, I decided to be funny and practical. I fashioned a note which I intended to affix to my derriere to convey my message to my doctor and make him laugh. On a sheet of copy paper, I typed an asterisk. Using the copier, I enlarged the asterisk until it was about an inch in diameter. Afterwards, I typed the following on the same sheet of paper, "Good morning, Dr. McGarvey. I know you are a good "assologyst." But I would like to make sure that my rectum opening will look like the one shown here after the surgery. I am looking forward to a good result. Thank you very much."

On the day of my surgery, I tried to attach the note to my behind using Scotch tape, but it kept coming off. I decided instead to hand him the note when he met me before the surgery. As soon as he read the note, he laughed and said, "Mickey, I understand both your request and your concern. But the best I can do for you is duplicate the shape of the Mercedes logo." Apparently, he enjoyed my joke, and we settled on the Mercedes logo. The surgery was successful, and I have not had any major hemorrhoid problems since then. Unfortunately, he was unable to duplicate the Mercedes logo he promised. I instead have something that resembles a Subaru logo.

Delta House

After breaking up with Joni and moving like a stray cat from one friend's apartment to another, I found a job washing dishes at a restaurant in downtown SLO called Luisa's Place. I was earning $1.95 an hour and was able to afford my own place.

I found a one-bedroom apartment which I shared with Takada-kun. As I wrote earlier, it evolved into a veritable Delta House. We always kept the front door unlocked, and our friends came and went.

Wall of Shame

One by one, our friends covered a 4' X 4' section of our dining room wall at Delta House with nude pictures they found in Playboy magazines. In one week, the entire wall was covered with nude photos.

When I returned from work one day, four of my friends were sitting in the dining room, admiring the wall of nude photos. They each had mischievous grins on their faces. Initially, I did not know what they had been up to. Then I traced the lines of their gazes back to the wall and found what they were grinning at.

They had found two nude photos of me and taped them to the wall. Joni had taken these photos of me in Nagano when I was lying completely nude in bed.

My Funeral

As usual, when I arrived home from work, I found my friends sitting in the dining room. This time, however, they did not say anything to me and just gazed down at the floor as if they were praying.

I finally realized what was happening. They had placed a 4" X 6" frame with my Cal Poly graduation photo on the window ledge with several vases of flowers around it. These guys were holding my funeral while I was still alive!

Luminous Paint Incident

We were having a party in our dining room one night, and everyone gathered there was pretty intoxicated and having a good time. All of a sudden, someone turned off the lights. I looked around and could not believe what I was seeing.

While Takada-kun and I were out, someone had painted the shapes of the moon, stars, and sexually provocative objects all over the ceiling and the walls in luminous paint. I later learned that the toilet seat cover was also painted. We were so intoxicated and stoned that night that we spent hours just looking at the walls and ceiling.

Takada-kun and I hoped that whoever moved in after us enjoyed the scenery as much as we did.

Louisa's Place

It was a small but busy restaurant started by Louisa Webb and her husband Frank in 1976. I was hired as a dishwasher in 1978. I worked from 7 a.m. until 3 a.m., five days a week. Even though Louisa knew that I had a degree from Cal Poly, she never questioned why I was washing dishes or asked about my immigration status. I believe that she liked my personality.

On any given day, in addition to Louisa, there were two waitresses, a cook, a dishwasher, and a kitchen helper working in the restaurant. I operated the dish washing machine next to Louisa and the kitchen helper, in the back of the restaurant. The waitress working in the front section of the restaurant typically earned $50 a day in tips, which was a substantial amount of money in 1978. During the breakfast and lunch hours, the restaurant was very busy. I worked quickly and efficiently, as always, and found time after washing the dishes to help the waitresses bus and set up the tables. I even worked the cash register when needed. Despite all the help I was giving the waitresses, they never shared their tips with me.

One day, Louisa asked the waitresses to share their tips with me, but the waitress who worked in the front section of the restaurant refused. A week later, Louisa fired her. Louisa and I got along very well, and she appreciated my sense of humor.

Six months later, Louisa asked me if I would clean the restaurant after it closed. She was willing to pay me $10 per night. I accepted. Soon after, she bought a much bigger restaurant near Madonna Inn, offering a similar menu. She asked me to clean that restaurant, too. I resigned from my dishwashing job since the income I was earning from cleaning the two restaurants gave me the freedom to do other things, mainly buying, fixing, and selling cars for a profit.

Autocross

Autocross is a timed competition where drivers navigate a course marked by pylons. If the course is small, only one driver at a time is permitted to race. Cars are categorized based on their engine size, modifications, and so on. This type of competition provides a safe racing environment.

I bought a 1968 four-door Datsun 510, the same type of car that Paul Newman used to race in. I invested a lot of money in the car to modify it into an autocross vehicle; however, I also maintained its street legal status. I installed a roll bar, rear disc brakes, front sway bar, rear adjustable sway bar, heavy duty shocks, a set of aluminum wheels with fat tires, and I did all the work myself.

I participated in the races held by the Cal Poly Auto Club and did fairly well. While the school was in session, the auto club closed off one of the large parking lots once a month on a weekend for autocross racing.

Keep on Rolling

There are some mistakes in life that are not worth repeating, but I apparently did not get the memo. During an autocross competition I needed to fuel my car, so I drove to a nearby gas station with Saito-kun as my passenger. On our way back to the autocross site, I started racing on a very wide two-lane street with the driver of a Ford Capri.

The road veered left and I entered the curve at seventy miles per hour. I mishandled my car and lost control of it. My Datsun 510 flipped over one and a half times, hit a hill head-on, and finally came to rest on its roof.

Fortunately, Saito-kun was not hurt, but I hit my head on the caved in roof. It sounds familiar, doesn't it?

The roll bar I had installed did not protect my side of the roof. Saito-kun went back to the autocross competition on foot. Another friend took me to the doctor to be examined. Luckily, I did not sustain any long-term injuries. My Datsun was towed to the parking lot of my apartment.

These days, I suffer from cervical spondylosis, commonly called degenerative arthritis of the neck. My current wife tells me that it was caused by all the stupid things that I did when I was young.

The Next Race Car

I needed a replacement for my totaled 1968 Datsun 510, and my roommate, Takada-kun, was ready to sell his flared, two-door, 1970 Datsun 510. I purchased it from him, and with my friends' help I transferred the salvageable parts from my wrecked car to the new car.

My new racecar was much nicer than the previous one with its bright orange paint and black interior. I raced it quite a bit before I sold it and bought a 1976 Nissan New Silvia (equivalent to a 1977 Datsun 200SX), which I purchased from a friend who was leaving for Japan. He had driven the car in Tokyo for a year and shipped it to SLO when he came to the U.S. to study. Since it was a Japanese car, the steering wheel was on the right side. The car got a lot of attention, and I enjoyed every minute of it.

My First Wife

I met my first wife, Alice, a brown-eyed blonde, at a dance club in SLO. It was a club where people as young as 18 were permitted entry. This was when disco music was very popular. Just about everyone had watched John Travolta's film, *Saturday Night Fever*. One of my friends had watched it ten times to learn John Travolta's dance routine.

Alice was from Staten Island. She moved to California with her mother, younger sister, and two female friends. Alice shared an apartment in SLO with her female friends. After we dated for about three months, I told her that if she lost ten pounds, I would marry her. Alice was not overweight at all, but she exercised on a stationary bike every day for a month and a half until she lost ten pounds.

Although I did not formally propose, Alice and I got married on August 11, 1979. We went to Honolulu for our honeymoon. At that time, Honolulu was not as crowded with tourists as it is today. We stayed at a low budget hotel right on the beach. When I say that the hotel was right on the beach, I mean it was right next to the water. When we went down the stairs, the ocean was at our feet.

The hotel did not have air conditioning, but we were staying on the sixth floor, so we left the windows wide open on those unbearably hot nights and let the strong wind cool the room down. Those trade winds were so strong that they blew the curtains all over the place.

Alice and I rented a Honda Civic and drove around the island of Oahu together, enjoying the sights and sounds. We returned to SLO after one week.

Our First Apartment

After returning from Hawaii, Alice and I settled into a one-bedroom apartment in SLO. She worked as an office clerk for a small airline company headquartered in SLO. In addition to cleaning the two restaurants Louisa owned, I supplemented our income by buying, fixing, and selling cars. I used the apartment's parking lot to work on these cars.

One day, while working on a 1972 Triumph Spitfire, the car's clamshell hood fell on my head like a guillotine. My head was trapped between the bottom edge of the hood and the car's body. I temporarily lost consciousness. Fortunately, I recovered and continued working on the car. My list of head injuries was getting longer.

Alice was an old-fashioned girl, and she really wanted to start a family as soon as possible. Soon after we married, Alice became pregnant.

My First Child

When Alice became pregnant, we moved into a nicer one-bedroom apartment in SLO. Our first child, Ann, was born on September 10, 1980. My father and my cousin came to visit us after our baby's birth.

I picked them up at Los Angeles International Airport in my 1975 Honda Accord. Before taking them to SLO, I showed them around Los Angeles and took them to Hollywood, where we visited an adult bookstore. My cousin's eyes popped wide open when he saw the various magazines featuring totally nude women, and the pornographic videos, the likes of which he had never imagined in Japan. He purchased a video and asked me to ship it to him in Nagano since he was concerned about getting caught with it in customs. I shipped the video to him after he had returned to Japan, but customs rejected it and shipped it back to me. My cousin was very disappointed, but his loss became my gain; I really enjoyed watching it.

We arrived at our apartment safely. After we finished dinner, I offered marijuana to my cousin and my father. I told them that weed was not as bad as Japanese people made it out to be. I showed them how to smoke it from a bong (water pipe). As I was about to take a second hit, my father reached over and took the bong from my hands and asked me to load it up. This really surprised me. I finally saw another side of him that I did not know. He took a couple of hits from the bong and appeared to get high. He seemed to enjoy it and probably concluded that pot was not as bad as he believed. My cousin, on the other hand, never smoked.

Career Transition

I resigned from cleaning Louisa's restaurants and began a short-lived career as a real estate agent. I couldn't have chosen a worst time to start working for Red Carpet Realty. The interest rates were over fifteen percent. During the eighteen months I was employed there, I only sold six houses.

Fortunately, we had $10,000 in our savings account and were earning $100 a month in interest income. I continued to buy, fix, and sell cars to supplement our earnings.

After I left the real estate industry, I was hired as a janitor at Cal Poly University. This coincided with the purchase of my first house. With my parents' help, I bought a three-bedroom home in Los Osos, merely twelve miles away from San Luis Obispo. The purchase price of the home was $72,000. My monthly mortgage payments were $580 plus the applicable real estate taxes.

New Job and Opportunity to Pursue a Second Degree

Alice and I were hired by Cal Poly University at nearly the same time. She obtained a job as a computer key punch operator. My gross income was a little over $1,000 a month, which was a big leap from what I had earned at Louisa's.

My shift started at 3:30 a.m. and ended at 11:30 a.m. I left our house in Los Osos at 3:00 a.m. to get to work. Each janitor was assigned to a specific area. If one of the janitors in our section did not show up for work, it was my responsibility to clean his or her area as well as mine. We all had a 4' X 9' station to store our cart and supplies. The station was equipped with a small desk and a chair, so we could do our paperwork.

We were allowed to take one class at Cal Poly during our work hours, and I took full advantage of it. I decided to get another Bachelor of Science degree, this time in computer science. However, I cheated the system. Instead of taking only one class, I took two classes a day without anyone knowing. I studied in the janitorial station and took a nap there for a few hours every day after cleaning my area. No one knew what I was doing, nor did they complain. I kept my area clean. I believe there were other janitors who slept in their stations as well.

I finished cleaning by 5:30 a.m. I used many techniques that other janitors did not, which allowed me to finish my job faster than the others. Rather than vacuuming the floors, I picked up the small debris by hand. Instead of sanitizing the toilets, I used plenty of paper towels to clean them and the floors surrounding them.

After a short breakfast break before 7 a.m., we were supposed to inspect our areas and perform other tasks, such as dusting and polishing the floors until 11:30 a.m. I seldom did this, and my boss never complained. Occasionally, he visited my station while I was taking a nap and let himself in using his master key. Sometimes I barricaded the door with my cart and hid myself among other things in the station so he would not catch me napping when he opened the door. Oftentimes, I wedged a long piece of wood under the door knob to prevent him from entering immediately. I was fairly sure that my boss knew what I was doing, but he never complained because I kept my assigned area in good shape.

Whenever I napped at my desk in my janitorial station, I placed both arms on the desk and laid my head on one arm while twisting my neck. I repeatedly slept this way for about three months, until my neck finally gave out. One day, I found that I could not turn my head sideways. I had to go to a chiropractor for three weeks before I could turn my head normally. I ultimately changed my sleeping habit to prevent further neck problems.

There was a lot of wildlife surrounding the Cal Poly campus. One day, I caught one trespassing in my area. It was a nasty opossum with sharp teeth, which he showed as he snarled at me. It took me thirty minutes to catch him in a bucket. I released him outside.

Married Life and Parenthood

Our daughter, Ann, was almost two when Alice and I were working at Cal Poly. Since I worked until 11:30 a.m., Alice dropped Ann off at the babysitter's house, a mile away, before she left for work. I picked up Ann up from the babysitter on my way home, around noon. Ann had already eaten lunch, so I let her play in the living room while I studied at the kitchen table. When Ann took a nap, I either took a nap myself or worked on cars.

Alice came home around 5:30 p.m. and prepared dinner. She never complained about cooking, even though she had a full-time job. Our typical meals consisted of beef or pork, mashed potatoes, macaroni and cheese, and some vegetables. The meals were delicious, but very high in saturated fat. I believe eating this way contributed to my high cholesterol levels. When I moved to Los Angeles, my doctor ordered a routine blood test. My total cholesterol was a whopping 305. I have been taking cholesterol-lowering medication ever since.

Legal Alien Status

Since Alice was a U.S. citizen, I decided to apply for a green card (officially known as a Permanent Resident Card). At that time, many illegal aliens entered into fake marriages to obtain permanent resident status, and I had been told that because of the number of fake marriages, the interviewer might ask very personal questions. I was fully prepared to answer them.

We drove 200 miles, with Ann, to the U.S. immigration office in downtown Los Angeles. But first we decided to stop at a nearby McDonald's to get something to eat.

While we were waiting in the long line at the restaurant, we were playing with Ann. I noticed a lady standing behind us and smiling pleasantly. We finished eating and headed to the immigration office. When we were called to meet with the immigration officer, we recognized that it was the same lady who had been standing behind us in line at McDonald's.

That encounter probably helped enforce the fact that our marriage was real. After just a few questions, the interview concluded.

Quitting is Not an Option

I am the type of person who always finishes what I start; quitting is not an option. This applied to the many cars I fixed and painted in my double garage.

I was working on the transmission of a Fiat X19 around midnight. While I attempted to install a spring washer that measured an inch in diameter, it somehow bounced up and hit me in my right eye. It was extremely painful. I went inside and examined my eye in the mirror. I was shocked to see that half of my eyeball had hemorrhaged and was covered in blood. I could barely see anything out of my right eye.

But, not being a quitter, I returned to the garage and continued working on the transmission for another hour with my right eye closed. When I woke up the following morning, some of the blood had disappeared. I went to see an eye doctor, nonetheless. After examining my eye, he told me that I was absolutely crazy. Fortunately, my eye completely recovered in three days.

Something for the Car Buffs

I had plenty of space in my double garage in Los Osos, so I took advantage of it and modified my Nissan New Silvia. I wanted to make it a highly competitive autocross vehicle.

I began by making four flared fenders for the car by hand. I used sheet metal, pop rivets, fiberglass, and plenty of Bondo body filler to construct them. Next, I painted the entire car bright red. Afterward, I lowered the rear end using a pair of three-inch lowering blocks and hand-made U-bolts. I installed a 2-liter engine block from a Datsun pickup truck along with a high-performance SSS cylinder head imported from Japan. I ported the cylinder head and installed a high-performance camshaft, valve springs, and camshaft oil spreader.

Over time, I added a pair of 45mm Weber carburetors, special air cleaners, a header, a brake balancer, a remote engine oil cooler, a high-performance ignition coil, a professionally calibrated distributor, high compression pistons, a strut bar with camber plates, a full roll cage (I bought a kit and installed it after gutting the whole interior), a Corbeau racing seat with a five-point safety harness, a heavy duty front sway bar with Teflon bushings, an adjustable rear sway bar, height adjustable front struts, rear disc brakes, and a limited slip differential, all of which gave me a competitive edge.

I earned a number of trophies competing at Cal Poly autocross events. After I moved to Los Angeles in 1986, I participated in autocross events sponsored by a local auto club once a month. In the street-modified class, I always placed in the top three but never won any races in that class. I occasionally competed in national events sponsored by the Sports Car Club of America (SCCA).

Car Trouble with My New Silvia

I drove my New Silvia 250 miles to Manzanar (the former site of an American concentration camp where Japanese Americans were incarcerated during World War II), to compete in an autocross event at an old airfield. I won the second-place trophy. After the award ceremony concluded at 8 p.m., I started my journey back home.

About 150 miles into the trip, I suddenly heard a loud noise coming from underneath the car. I managed to find a gas station near the freeway off ramp and pulled over. I was totally shocked to see that the exhaust pipe, which had been connected to the exhaust header flange, had separated and was dragging on the freeway. Because of the vibrations, the three bolts holding them together were dislodged. I was carrying a lot of tools in my trunk, but without the lost bolts, the tools were useless.

I had to think fast. I saw an opening in the transmission tunnel, threaded a battery jumper cable through it, and looped it around the hanging pipe. I brought the looped ends inside the car and placed them next to my driver's seat. Once seated inside the car, I placed cigarette butts in my ears and put on my racing helmet. I started the engine and grabbed the jumper cable with my left hand. With my right hand on the steering wheel, I started driving. Remember, the steering wheel was on the right side of this Japanese-imported car.

The noises were still unbearable. Driving 150 miles while holding the cable was also very tiring. I was fortunate that I wasn't pulled over by the police for excessive noise in the middle of the night. I got home without further incident. After participating in a few more races, I reached the conclusion that I had no talent for driving a race car competitively. I eventually converted the New Silvia back to a street legal vehicle and sold it for $1,800. In the twenty years during which I owned this car, I had painted it three times and spent at least $40,000 on upgrades. It seemed a shame to let it go for so little money, but I had enjoyed working on the car and racing it.

My Marriage on the Rocks

My wife's life ambition was to stay at home and raise a family. Our values did not match. I did not want to remain a janitor all my life with a bachelor's degree in business management. I wanted to pursue a second degree in computer science, which I thought would be a good money-making field in the future.

In addition to the two classes I was taking during work hours, I attended two computer classes per week while taking care of our daughter after work. I reserved my time on weekends for fixing cars to supplement our income.

Sometimes, Alice spontaneously asked me to go to a movie the next day. I repeatedly asked her to tell me at least a week in advance so I could plan my schedule accordingly. This did not make her happy. Although I understood how she felt, I did not know how to handle the situation.

xvi. On the race course with the New Silvia

When Alice was pregnant with our second child, Lynn, we got into a big argument, even though Alice was not the type of person who became outraged. After the fight, I got into my 1970 Datsun Roadster and disappeared for two days without telling her where I was going. Based on my past history, it might be easy to guess that I drove 400 miles to Reno and gambled. I stayed there for one night and drove back. I don't recall how much money I lost. Naturally, Alice was not happy about the way I behaved.

Alice Files for Divorce

About three months after this incident, I was coming out of the office where I clocked out. I saw a young lady looking at me. She approached me, and after confirming my name, she handed me a piece of paper.

At first, I thought it was a love letter, but it turned out to be a divorce paper. It was March 11, 1983, my 31st birthday. I asked myself, "Why on my birthday?" I never asked her why she chose my birthday to serve me with the divorce paper. I was devastated and decided to move out of our marital home in Los Osos and look for a new place to live. Our second child, Lynn, was born on June 28, 1983.

Trouble Brewing

I moved into a room in a house I shared with three other roommates. The owner of the house, Ethan, lived in the converted garage he shared with his girlfriend. Ethan was my age, and he was a masonry worker. My rent was $190 a month, and Ethan collected one month's rent as a security deposit.

I visited Alice, Ann, and our newborn baby, Lynn, as often as I could. Even though I owned the house in Los Osos, I let Alice and the kids live there until I moved to Los Angeles in 1986, when I had no other choice but to sell it. During the time Alice lived in the house, I paid the mortgage loan and property taxes, and I gave her $300 for child support. I also mowed the lawn every weekend.

I don't remember how I managed to survive on the $900 I was bringing home every month when I was paying $580 for the mortgage, $300 for child support, and $190 for rent and other expenses. After living in Ethan's house for eighteen months I decided to move out. I did not have another place lined up. I gave him one month's notice, and we verbally agreed that I could use the security deposit to cover the last month's rent.

Trouble

One day, while I was still looking for a new place to live, Ethan came into the living room. I was helping his friend, Richard, with something. Ethan started complaining that he had not received my rent payment for the last month. I reminded him that we had agreed to use my security deposit for last month's rent. Ethan denied making that agreement with me. He was an excitable individual and started yelling at me.

The argument spilled over to the backyard, where all of a sudden, he attacked me physically. He held me in a headlock, but I knew I could take him down using a judo technique. Ethan was 5'10" and weighed 180 pounds, whereas I was 5'7" and weighed 150 pounds. I still knew I could take him down, but I saw a big glass wall just a few feet from where we were standing. I thought that if I took him down using a judo move, we could potentially fall through the glass wall and someone could get hurt. While I was debating whether or not to use the judo move, Ethan suddenly jerked me up and gave me a sucker punch that landed on the tip of my chin. I briefly knelt down on my knee until I got my bearings back. Ethan walked away ten feet from where I was kneeling.

My temper flared. I tried to go after Ethan, but one of his friends, Tommy, was standing outside watching this unfold. He stepped in between Ethan and me and said, "If you want to fight Ethan, you have to go through me first." Tommy was even bigger than Ethan at 6'1" and at least 220 pounds.

At that moment, Richard came out of the house, grabbed me, and took me inside. I went into the kitchen and spat blood into the kitchen sink. I also noticed that I was unable to speak. I went into the bathroom to check my jaw in the mirror. I moved my lower lip down with my fingers and noticed a red line running down the middle of my lower gum line. I found that I could speak by holding both sides of my jaw with my fingers. It was obvious that my jaw was broken. Richard drove me to the emergency room. I called Alice and told her what had happened while holding both sides of my jaw in order to speak.

The doctor decided to operate on my broken jaw right away. My jaw was broken in two places.

After Jaw Surgery

The next morning, I went into the bathroom to see myself in the mirror. I found that the medical staff had not done a good job of cleaning me up after the surgery. There was blood all over my neck and my hair. When I returned to my hospital bed, the staff brought breakfast for me and my roommate. When I saw the food, I was stunned. Other than the beverage, everything on the tray was solid food. I could do nothing but sit there and stare at the food for ten minutes.

My roommate sensed there was something wrong and asked what brought me to the hospital. I pointed to my jaw, and he figured out that I had a broken jaw and called for a nurse. A nurse came in and apologized for their mistake and brought me something I could drink through a straw.

I was discharged the same day and went to Alice's house, because I had nowhere else to go. I knew I could not stay there too long, so I started looking through the local newspaper classifieds and calling people. My jaw was completely wired shut with stainless steel wires, and I was in a great deal of pain. Talking with both my upper and lower teeth wired together was impossible, but I tried nevertheless. Some people hung up on me right away as I started to speak. I must have called six people. Finally, I found one person who showed some compassion and was willing to listen to me.

That was how I eventually found a new place to live. It was a two-bedroom apartment that I shared with a Cal Poly student, Ralph. One week after the surgery, I went to my old place to retrieve some items from my room. When I parked my car in front of Ethan's house, I saw Tommy standing outside, doing something on the side of the house. As soon as he saw me get out of my car, his face turned completely ashen as if he had seen a ghost. He must have thought that I returned to seek revenge, possibly with a gun. He sheepishly said, "Hi," but I ignored him and took care of my business.

Recovery

One week after my surgery, I went to the doctor for a checkup. He was happy to see that I was making progress and advised me that it would take at least another six weeks for me to make a full recovery. In the meantime, I was drinking five cans of strawberry or vanilla shakes a day. By the time I fully recovered, I had lost eight pounds.

I went to visit the doctor in another four weeks (the fifth week after surgery), and he removed two wires each from the top and bottom of my jaw. These wires were imbedded between my teeth. When he pulled them out, it caused me excruciating pain, even though he sprayed numbing medication on my gums. Eight wires remained, and he planned to remove them on the seventh week after the surgery. I remembered the pain I experienced on my last visit to that doctor and did not want to endure it again. The night before I was supposed to see the doctor for the last time, I sat at the desk in my room with a mirror in front of me. With a pair of long nose pliers and a wire cutter, I cut one wire at a time, straightened it, and pulled it out while trying not to cause myself too much pain. Unless I cut the wire properly, the sharp edge caused me excruciating pain when it passed through my gum line. As I removed the wires, tears welled up in my eyes and my mouth filled with blood. I struggled for more than 40 minutes to pull out six of the remaining eight wires, leaving just two wires for the doctor to remove.

I thought that the doctor would get mad at me if I removed all the wires. When I finally saw the doctor, he told me that no patient of his had ever removed the wires on his or her own. When I came home after the doctor removed the last two wires, I could barely open my mouth. I started worrying that I would never be able to fully open my mouth again. However, after one week, I was able to open my mouth like a crocodile.

Lawsuit

As a victim of violent crime, I filed for compensation with the state of California, which paid all my hospital and medical bills, even though I had good insurance coverage provided by my employer, Cal Poly.

Next, I hired a lawyer, who just happened to live next door to Ethan. After I explained what had happened, he took my case immediately, saying, "I cannot stand a big guy beating on a small guy like you." The lawyer was about my size.

We settled with Ethan's home owner's insurance company for $14,500. After the bills were paid, I received a little over sixty percent of the settlement. After this incident, I joked with people that if they gave me $10,000, I would let them break my arm. I was still just as crazy as before.

xvii. Kris and I on our wedding day, Las Vegas (October 4, 2011)

Los Angeles

1986 – Present

Heading to Los Angeles

After I earned my second Bachelor of Science degree in computer science, Endo-kun and I decided to move to Los Angeles. There would be more employment opportunities in Los Angeles. Even though I really hated the idea of living so far away from my daughters, it was a decision I had to make for my future.

We loaded up my 1970 Datsun pickup truck with everything that we owned and left San Luis Obispo. To say that the trip was normal and uneventful would be a gross understatement. As soon as we got on the freeway, we realized the truck was swaying dangerously from side to side. We were forced to get off the freeway and went to a nearby gas station, where we found that the tires were underinflated. Another reason the truck swayed was that we had overloaded it with our belongings. Once the tires were properly inflated, we got back on the freeway.

About one hour into our trip, I needed to answer nature's call. I parked my pickup truck on the side of the freeway and carefully descended the thirty-degree slope, which was covered with lots of bushes and rocks. After I descended about ten feet, I found a good spot. As luck would have it, my foot slipped as I was taking care of business and I tumbled another ten feet down the slope. It happened all of a sudden, and I did not even have the opportunity to zip up my pants. Fortunately, nothing hanging out was injured, but I felt a sharp pain in my right ankle. I thought perhaps I had broken it during my fall, but a more urgent matter occupied my thoughts. Somehow, I managed to get up and finished my business while standing on one leg, imitating the pose actor Ralph Macchio made famous in the 1984 film, *The Karate Kid*.

I crawled back up the slope to my pickup truck and I asked Endo-kun to take over driving. We stopped at a gas station in Santa Barbara to check my ankle. Fortunately, it did not appear to be broken, just sprained.

We stayed at a friend's house in Gardena for a few days, then we found a two-bedroom apartment in Lawndale. It was a convenient location just five miles from Los Angeles International Airport. A week later, I drove my pickup truck back to Los Osos to get my New Silvia. I already had a buyer for the pickup truck.

Life in Lawndale

Once Endo-kun and I settled in our new apartment, we played golf every afternoon at a nearby nine-hole golf course. It cost $2. After three weeks of enjoying a relaxed lifestyle, we knew we had to get serious about finding jobs. I found a cheap Ford Capri for him to drive around in. Then I registered with a Japanese employment agency while Endo-kun combed through the newspaper want ads.

He was the first of us to find a job and became a floor manager at a new downtown Japanese sushi restaurant called Sushi Tron. It employed the latest technology, which enabled customers to place their orders using a touch screen. Many of those who patronized the restaurant were flight attendants for Japan Airlines and All Nippon Airways. Because of his friendly nature, Endo-kun did very well on the job.

Soon after I registered with the Japanese employment agency, I received a call to go on a job interview with a Japanese company located in Anaheim, about a 42-mile drive from Lawndale. The firm offered me a position as an office manager, which I accepted.

It was a small office of three employees in addition to me. The company sold Japanese-made wafer exposure machines and their related parts to affiliated companies. The pay was fairly decent, but the job itself was boring. On top of that, the long commute to and from work was exhausting. I drove nearly 85 miles round trip each day. By the time I arrived back home, I only had enough energy to eat and go to sleep.

Robbed!

We lived on the second floor of the apartment complex, and our unit was located on the north end. There was an exterior metal staircase we used to access our apartment. I came home from work one day and parked my car in the street. As I climbed up the third or fourth step of the metal staircase, I heard a noise that sounded like someone leaping onto the floor. I didn't pay much attention to it. Then, when I came to the front door of our apartment, I noticed that the window next to the door was half open and the glass was broken. At that moment, I realized that we had been burglarized. The thief must have jumped through the open window and escaped when he heard my footsteps on the staircase.

I was unsure if anyone was still inside our apartment, so I slowly opened the front door, but I couldn't see inside very well. I crouched down in a karate stance and slowly approached our rooms. No one was there. I felt relieved that I did not have to use my karate and judo talents.

When Endo-kun returned home, he inspected his room and confirmed that nothing was missing. I was not as lucky. The thief stole my $2,000 video camera, a gift from my cousin when he and my father visited me in San Luis Obispo. He also stole about $30 in small change.

I contacted the police, but there was nothing they could do. I also reached out to the landlord to have the broken window glass replaced. This was our introduction to big city living.

Las Vegas Road Trip

Endo-kun and I decided to take a road trip to Vegas in his Ford Capri. Las Vegas was only 285 miles from Lawndale. We embarked on our journey in the middle of summer, and the car did not have air conditioning. After the first 190 miles, the inside of the car felt like a hot oven. From that point on, it seemed that the temperature inside the car increased by one degree for every mile we drove.

The car was traveling at a speed of 85 miles per hour, but the breeze coming through the open windows was not helping. It felt like the hot air rushing out of an oven when you open an oven door. We thought we were heading to hell.

We arrived in Vegas in one piece and went straight to the blackjack tables. I don't recall how much money we lost, but we definitely lost. On the drive back to Los Angeles, we experienced the same kind of hell. Endo-kun's car broke down one week after we returned from Las Vegas.

The Bus Gambling Trip to Vegas

I got the idea to take a bus to Las Vegas. I found one that would drop me off right at the casino, and with three hundred dollars in my pocket, I boarded the bus. Most of the passengers were elderly, but that did not bother me.

When we reached our destination, we had ten hours to enjoy Vegas any way we wanted before heading back to Los Angeles. I disembarked full of excitement and anticipation and headed straight to the blackjack tables. I started gambling, and at one point I was actually ahead by a few hundred dollars. After five hours I managed to lose it all. I was at a loss as to how I should spend the remaining five hours before the bus departed for Los Angeles. I was so desperate that I went into the bar with my driver's license in hand and asked the bar patrons if they could lend me money, promising that I would pay them back once I returned to Los Angeles. In retrospect, I know I behaved in a disgraceful manner, but at the time I was a crazy gambler and an addict who was not bothered by what I did to get money.

Since I was unsuccessful at the bar, I approached the casino's pit bosses and asked them to loan me some money. One of them told me that he would help me if I could find the dealer who had witnessed me winning a few hundred dollars earlier. To my dismay, I could not find her. I spent the next five hours walking around the casino like a zombie. Given my past experiences, I was lucky to have a ride back home this time.

New Used Cars for Both of Us

After Endo-kun and I started earning steady incomes, we were able to save money. I purchased a 1977 Mazda RX7 for commuting, and Endo-kun bought a white 1976 Pontiac Trans Am.

I parked the RX7 and the New Silvia on the street. As I was getting into my RX7 one morning, I noticed that the left rear flared fender of the New Silvia was smashed in and the big whale tail mounted on the rear trunk lid was torn. I was devastated, and I felt violated. There were pieces of Bondo body filler and red paint scattered all over the pavement. It was obviously a hit and run accident, and it must have happened during the night. I fixed the damage myself and removed the whale tail from the rear trunk lid.

Alice and My Daughters

One year after I moved to Los Angeles, Alice informed me that she was moving to Rohnert Park with her mother, who was planning to pursue a counseling degree at Sonoma State University. Hearing the news devastated me. Rohnert Park is located forty miles northeast of San Francisco and 425 miles from Los Angeles. When they lived in San Luis Obispo, I only had to drive 200 miles from Los Angeles to see my kids on the spur of the moment. Now, that opportunity was being taken away from me.

However, I continued to send Alice $600 a month for child support until my girls reached age eighteen. I also called them once a week in an effort to stay in touch with them. I was not able to see them as often as I wanted to, but I made the 850-mile drive roundtrip to see them when I could.

Throughout the years, and well into their adulthood, I continued helping my daughters financially with tuition payments, buying cars, and eventually buying houses. I wanted to help my children as much as my parents had helped me. To this day, Ann and Lynn continue to call me for assistance with various scenarios, including seeking my advice on legal matters. I am always willing to help them.

Redondo Beach

In 1987, Endo-kun moved out of the apartment we shared together. His girlfriend, whom he had been seeing when he filed for a divorce, came to America to live with him. They found a nice house in Torrance and moved in together.

After he moved out, I needed to find another place to live. Again, with my parents' help, I purchased a two-bedroom, 1,500 square-foot townhouse in Redondo Beach, just one mile from the Pacific Ocean. I liked the fact that it had a double garage where I could fix cars.

One year after moving to Torrance together, Endo-kun and his girlfriend married. They had a very nice wedding. Endo-kun found a better paying job as a sales manager for a Japanese moving company. Since he was a very personable man, he was successful in drawing in clients. He continued to work for that company until he and his wife decided to return to Japan, where they wanted to raise their two children.

They lived in Torrance for about seven or eight years. I frequently visited them during the weekends, and they often prepared me nice dinners. Endo-kun and I, along with two other SLO friends, have remained in touch over the years. With recent technological developments, we meet over Zoom every three months.

It has been thirty-six years since I moved to Redondo Beach, and I still live in the same townhouse. I no longer want to go through the hassle of moving. When I first purchased the place, it had a jacuzzi on the patio, and I hosted a lot of parties around it. However, since the previous owner had installed the jacuzzi illegally, I was forced to get rid of it.

Other than the time I was married, I always shared the townhouse with a female roommate in an effort to offset my living expenses. Until I got married for the third time, I had had ten female roommates. I chose to have female roommates because they are less destructive than men and they have a tendency to spend time at their boyfriend's homes. All of my roommates were good, with the exception of an office worker in her late twenties. When she moved out, I was absolutely shocked by how filthy her room and bathroom were.

Roommate's Crazy Boyfriend

One of my former roommates was in her mid-twenties when we lived together, and she had a boyfriend who was around her age, named Gary. We all got along well and did things together. One day, we decided to take a day trip to Rosarito, Mexico.

Rosarito is located ten miles south of the U.S.-Mexico border. The three of us piled into my car and drove down to a beach in Rosarito. When we arrived, we saw a crowd of young people gathered on the beach and they were having fun. There was also a large stage on the beach for dancing, bands, and other events.

Soon after we arrived, we heard an announcement that there were going to be push-up and rope pulling contests. Gary and I decided to participate in both events. The push-up contest organizers formed two groups consisting of four people each. Gary and I were in the first group. As we lined up on the stage, we saw that a large group of spectators had gathered to watch us.

The master of ceremonies began counting. As he counted, we were supposed to do one push-up per count and our chests were supposed to touch or come very close to the stage floor. There were two muscular guys in our group who dropped out after the count of twenty. Gary dropped out at the count of forty-five, but I was still going strong. When the count reached eighty-two, I was forced to drop out since I could not maintain one push-up per count. I was declared the winner of the first group.

The second group took the stage, and three of the guys dropped out after the count reached thirty. One guy continued to do push-ups, but he noticeably slowed down after the count of sixty-five. However, the master of ceremonies allowed him to continue. After seeing this, I shouted, "That's cheating!" His chest was not even close to the stage floor. Ultimately, he managed to reach the count of eighty-three and was declared the winner. This really angered me. I was given a pitcher of margaritas for finishing in second place.

Half an hour later, we participated in the rope pulling contest. Gary and I competed in the second group. Gary was 5'9" and weighed 165 pounds. I was 5'7" and weighed 160 pounds. We competed against two American gorillas who were over six feet tall and weighed 200 pounds each.

Everyone thought that we would be no match for them, with our 325 pounds competing against their 400.

Gary and I managed to hold our positions for sixty seconds without giving them an inch, but we could not overcome the weight disadvantage. We eventually lost, but we were happy that we fought hard against those 200-pound monsters.

An hour later, music started playing and everyone jumped on the stage and started dancing. I had never seen anything like it. Later on, I learned that what they were doing was the Macarena. My roommate and Gary urged me to join them on stage, but I hesitated. After further coaxing, I got up on the stage. I tried to imitate the dance routine as much as I could, but I decided to dance my own way – my usual, crazy octopus dance. I did not know what people around me thought of me, but I had a hell of a good time.

One day, Gary and I were driving our cars toward my townhouse. He was driving in front in a beat-up MG convertible with its top down. The railway crossing arm came down, and we stopped and waited for the train to pass. It was a long cargo train moving at a very slow rate, probably only five miles per hour. All of a sudden, I saw Gary get out of his car and run toward the moving train cars with both their side doors totally open. He jumped on one of the train cars, crossed its entire width, and jumped out of it on the other side. He saw another car passing by and did exactly the same thing on his way back. He ran back and calmly got into his car. I knew he was athletic since we had practiced karate together a few times, but I never knew he was that crazy.

A few months after that incident, my roommate and Gary broke up. He was upset and came by the townhouse, where he threw a rock at the window of the room where she was staying. My roommate paid to have the broken glass replaced and moved out soon after. I never heard from either of them again.

New Job in Compton

Driving to work in Anaheim each day became unbearable, and I resigned in 1987. I registered with the Japanese employment agency once again. A week later, they contacted me and said they had a position for me with a Japanese company in Compton, which is only ten miles from Redondo Beach. I was interviewed by the general manager and hired as a salesperson.

The company sold imitations of the Sony Walkman, boomboxes, and car stereos manufactured by its parent company in Japan. The firm imported at least five full containers of merchandise from Japan each month and stored the merchandise in a giant warehouse. The least expensive version of the imitation Walkman was purchased from Japan for less than $6. It sold for less than $10 at Circuit City and other electronic goods retailers. Since the products were manufactured using substandard parts, we often had complaints, and the merchandise was returned to us.

The parent company in Japan sent the company president, Mr. Shinoda, and a few others to the United States. Mr. Shinoda had a very strange management style. He started the day by greeting the employees, about twenty-five in all, who assembled in a large room. Afterward, all ten of the sales personnel gathered in the meeting room and discussed the question Mr. Shinoda had assigned to the team the day before. The questions were related to sales and the products we had to sell. During the meeting, he spent an hour asking each and every one of us to answer the same question. Many of us felt that these meetings were useless and a complete waste of time.

Every three months, he announced an organizational change during his morning greeting. I worked there for a year and a half and had four different job titles: salesperson, warehouse manager, IT manager, and merchandise return manager.

The only saving grace was that I earned $3,600 a month at this company, which was $1,400 more than I earned at the job in Anaheim.

More About Mr. Shinoda

Mr. Shinoda had a beautiful Japanese wife, and they lived in a nice, company-provided house in Torrance. Employees sent to the United States by their parent companies in Japan earned a lot of money and were given many perks, such as company-provided houses and cars. We all believed that Mr. Shinoda was earning at least $12,000 per month.

One day, I asked him why he had hired me. His response was, "I saw you leaving through the front door after your interview, and I really liked how you looked from behind. You looked like someone who had guts!" Later, he learned that I could play mahjong, and he invited me and two other employees to his house to play.

His wife was an excellent cook. Every time we went there, normally on Friday night after work, there was a delicious Japanese meal waiting for us. We started playing mahjong after dinner and sometimes played straight through the night. Each game lasted ten minutes, and each player could lose as much as $30 per game. I was never a good gambler, and I lost about $2,500 in two months. I finally asked Mr. Shinoda not to invite me to join his mahjong game, which he did not appreciate.

I was looking for him one day and went into his large office, where I found a couple of Playboy magazines in his bathroom. I lost respect for him after that.

Sex Counselor

There was a Japanese girl in her mid-twenties who worked for the company's general manager. We talked once in a while and became friendly. She invited me into a small room one day and asked me for some very personal advice.

She told me that she was dating an American guy who was very well-endowed. Apparently, having sex with him was very painful for her, and she asked me what she should do. Of course, I was completely stunned by her question and wondered what made her think I was qualified to answer it.

Perhaps, in her eyes, I looked like someone with vast sexual experience, or she might have thought I was a well-endowed individual. Despite my shock, I did not want to disappoint her. I made some comments about what she should do and told her to use a lot of lubricant. She never approached me for follow-up advice.

Demise of the Company

With the popularity of imitation Walkman devices waning, several people in the company thought Mr. Shinoda was issuing fake invoices and doing other unethical things to meet the quotas imposed by the parent company in Japan.

I could see that the company's demise was imminent, so I resigned in October 1988. In less than a year, the company folded.

Dating Service in Santa Monica

When I moved to Los Angeles, I registered with a dating service in Santa Monica. I purchased a perpetual membership for $1,200, which would remain valid until I got married.

In 1987, I met a red-headed lady in her early thirties through the dating service. We hit it off very well. She and I participated in my company-sponsored trip to Maui, for which the company paid half of her expenses. Not long after that, we decided to get married, and I gave her an engagement ring. She was arranging everything for the wedding including the church, reception, and invitations.

One evening, we had a big argument on the phone, and she really got upset with me. I do not remember what the fight was about. Apparently, just before she hung up the phone, she removed my engagement ring and threw it into the bushes. I tried to get in touch with her later, but she refused to answer the phone. Eventually, I gave up.

I have no idea if she tried to find the engagement ring afterwards or whether she sold it. In hindsight, I am glad that I did not marry her. She was so temperamental that our marriage would never have worked out.

After our relationship ended, I met many other ladies through the dating service.

I Took my Daughters to Nagano

In 1988, I took my daughters, Ann (8) and Lynn (6), to Nagano for the first time. I wanted them to see their grandparents and the town I grew up in. We arrived on July 8 and stayed through July 17. I introduced Ann and Lynn to some of my relatives. They were very excited to see my girls, particularly my cousin's family who only lived a quarter of a mile away from my parents' house. My cousin is six years older than I, and he lives in the main Ohkubo family home he had inherited from his father. They welcomed the three of us with a big barbeque party followed by fireworks.

They took us to the summer festival in town, where the streets were overflowing with people. Many of the people we encountered, especially the kids, were excited to see Ann. She had blondish hair and hazel eyes, and few local people had come face-to-face with foreigners at that time.

I took my children to many places in Nagano, such as Zenkoji Temple, a museum, a dinosaur park, and an amusement park by the lake. Zenkoji Temple is one of the most frequently visited temples in Japan.

Among the girls' most favorite places was Karuizawa, which was, and still is, a popular summer holiday destination. It is the town John Lennon and his wife Yoko Ono often visited while in Japan.

A friend of mine picked us up at my parents' house and drove us to Karuizawa, which was about thirty-five miles from my parents' house. He guided us around town and took us to nearby Onioshidashi Volcanic Park. Located on the foot of Mount Asama volcano, the park features several walking paths in a landscape formed by ancient volcanic debris and rocks. There are various souvenir and food stands throughout the park.

Before we purchased any food at the food stand, the vendor offered me a sample. I thought this would be a good time to show my daughters my funny side and break them in, so to speak. So, as soon as I put the sample piece in my mouth and chewed a few times, I fell to the ground and pretended that I was choking on the food. While on the ground, I squinted my eyes and looked at my friend and my daughters. They all looked shocked by what was happening and did not seem to know what to do with me. I did not wish to make them suffer any longer, so, after ten seconds of acting, I stood up and told them that the food had passed through my throat and I was fine. I believe they knew I was faking. Anyway, my daughters were properly initiated by my joke.

After visiting Onioshidashi Volcanic Park, my friend drove us to the hilly side of town, where we got out of the car. We walked a short distance and reached Karuizawa Shiraito Falls, where John Lennon and Yoko Ono had their photo taken. After this, he drove us to a hotel that he had reserved for us and paid for. It was a very nice hotel suite with a large living room and two bedrooms. He returned the next day, picked us up in his car, and drove us back to my parents' house.

A couple of days after returning from Karuizawa, I took the girls to a supermarket and played a similar joke on them. This time, instead of falling to the ground, as soon as I placed the sample piece of food in my mouth, I made a very awkward face like I ate something that tasted very bad. The unfortunate person who gave me the sample did not know what to do with me. She simply asked me, "Is it bad?" I just left without saying anything with my daughters in tow.

Japanese people are very conservative, and I am among the few, if not the only person, who would do what I did with a straight face. A week later, I took my daughters to a different supermarket, and they stayed ten feet behind me. They had learned about their crazy father.

Five years later, I reinforced their training. Ann was thirteen and Lynn was eleven years old when they came to visit me in Redondo Beach. Ann needed to go to the store to buy feminine pads. I took her to a neighborhood Von's, a Southern California supermarket chain. When we arrived, I asked a store clerk where we could find them. The clerk guided us to the aisle and pointed to the proper section. While he was still with us, I asked Ann in a loud voice, "Do you want the ones with big wings or regular?"

Ann was embarrassed by my comment and blushed. We picked up what she wanted and brought the package to the cashier, where I asked her, "Aaaaaannn, don't you need the kind with the wings? Are you sure you don't need the kind with the wings?" The look on Ann's face told me that she wanted to run and get away from that scene as soon as possible. Since that incident, she has avoided going to stores with me.

Job Hunting

After I resigned from the job in Compton, my mother told me that the Nagano-based company I had previously worked for in 1977 was coming to Torrance to expand its business to the U.S. market. Immediately, I called the vice president who had hired me back then. He had become the company's president. He was glad that I called him and told me that he was looking for someone he could put in charge of the U.S. manufacturing section.

I flew to Japan, and we met at his company on November 3, 1988. He hired me, on the spot, as a general manager without any ill feelings about my abrupt resignation eleven years earlier. He set my starting salary at $4,000 a month.

At that time, the company had purchased a 25,000 square-foot building and completed the renovations on it. One side of the building was occupied by the sales division, but the manufacturing side was still empty. When I arrived for my first day of work on November 15, the manufacturing side consisted of a warehouse, a manufacturing area, and an office. The phone system was already installed, but there were only a desk and a chair in the office area. I had to purchase everything from furniture to office supplies. I also hired a secretary.

I assembled the partitions to make cubicles for the four Japanese employees, who were scheduled to arrive from Japan in two weeks. All of them were in their late twenties. Once they arrived, I was responsible for helping them obtain their social security cards, driver's licenses, insurance, and living quarters, among other things.

One of the employees brought his wife and baby with him. After he had been in the U.S. for eight months, he began to show some early signs of depression. I think this was due to the enormous pressure he felt to perform his job well and the responsibilities he had for his wife and baby. He had graduated from my high school, so he was a very bright individual.

I should have sent him to a doctor, but instead I jokingly gave him some advice. I told him to pleasure himself in the middle of the night and run a few blocks to relieve his stress. The next morning, he came to work looking even more depressed than before. When I asked him what happened, he responded, "Mickey-san. I did what you asked me to do last night, but it did not work." He was an intelligent person, but I could not believe he actually followed my silly advice. A month later, he decided to return to Japan.

As I wrote earlier, this company manufactured medical devices used in hospital labs. We assembled these devices using the parts manufactured by the parent company in Nagano and sold them to the sales division. The actual assembly work started in February 1989.

I worked at this company from 1988 to 2002, when it merged with another company.

The Airless Degreaser

In 1988, our parent company in Japan used vacuum technology to create an innovative, solvent-based cleaning machine for degreasing parts. Over the course of a few years, the company managed to sell a lot of the machines in Japan.

We called the machine the airless degreaser, and I wrote an article about it, titled "An Airtight Argument," which was published in the January 1999 edition of *Precision Cleaning* magazine.

The New Sales Manager

In 1990, I was asked to become a sales manager. The company wanted me to sell the new airless degreaser in the U.S. after its success in Japan. I tried to decline the position by telling them that I was afraid of flying. My futile attempts did not work, and I became the sales manager.

I did everything I could think of to promote the machine, including advertising it in specialty magazines, trade shows, direct mail advertising, cold calls, and word-of-mouth. It was very challenging to sell a machine with a price tag of over $100,000, especially when the conventional degreaser sold for as little as $20,000.

Fitness Club Member

In 1992, I joined a fitness club in Torrance. It was a fairly large club equipped with weight rooms, stationary bikes, a handball court, a pool, and an aerobics area. I went there every other day, lifted weights, and participated in an aerobics class. I really enjoyed working out there.

xviii. With my 1979 Porsche 911 (Slant Nose), circa 1992

After the club merged with Bally Total Fitness, it relocated to a much larger facility in Manhattan Beach. I lifted weights for 45 minutes, after which I took an advanced aerobics class for an hour. The aerobics classes were popular, especially on weekends, when the large room was packed with people. The weekday afternoons were not as crowded, so that was when I participated in the classes.

I was 44 then, and one of the oldest participants in the classes. However, my age did not discourage me from jumping higher than anyone else in the class. I thought I was doing the aerobics routine graciously, but in the other participants' eyes, I might have looked like an octopus doing aerobics. By this time, all of the octopuses in the world might be pleading with me not to degrade them by comparing my movements to theirs.

I am the type of person who hates to lose to anyone, no matter how young or athletic that person might be. There were a lot of young girls in my aerobics classes, and whenever I kicked my legs high, they tried to compete with me and kick higher. But they could never surpass me as I kicked my legs three inches above my head. However, I did not realize that my stubborn, competitive nature would cause one of my lumbar discs to rupture in 1998.

xix. Aboard the Battleship USS Iowa in San Pedro, California

In peak condition, I weighed 173 pounds and I could bench-press 260 pounds ten times. Sometimes I spotted a big guy bench-pressing 225 pounds and struggling with it. I deliberately asked him if I could work out with him on the same bench. When it was my turn, I easily lifted the same weight he was struggling with, ten times, after declining his offer to be my spotter. His facial expression was priceless, and I reveled in it.

Another thing that gave me great joy was watching the young girls work out in the aerobics classes. After spending 45 minutes lifting weights and 60 minutes in an aerobics class, I forced myself to get on the stationary bike placed directly behind the aerobics classroom. There, my view was not obstructed. I pedaled the stationary bike for 60 minutes while enjoying the view.

Around this time, during the weekends, I rode my mountain bike on The Strand, a lively beachfront sidewalk that attracts bicyclists, joggers, rollerbladers, and anyone out for a scenic stroll. The Strand connects the various Southern California beaches, and I sometimes rode from Hermosa Beach to Malibu, over 20 miles away.

Occasionally, while I was pedaling pretty hard, a group of young riders on their racing bikes passed me, triggering my competitive side. Immediately, I chased them as hard as I could. After half a mile or so, however, I found that I could not keep up with them because they were much younger, trained, and on their racing bikes. I slowed down my physical activities as I aged.

Met my Second Wife Through a Dating Service

I met my second wife, Jennifer, in 1993 through a dating service. On our first date, I picked her up at her one-bedroom apartment and we had dinner at a nice restaurant. Afterward, we went to a movie. She told me that she was originally from Kansas and employed as an architect.

After dating for three months, I asked Jennifer to move in with me. I placed everything she owned in my car trailer and brought it to my townhouse. She did not have very much at all. A few months after we began living together, we decided to get married. I was 40, and she was seven years my junior.

Jennifer's father came from Kansas to attend our wedding. The day before the wedding, he asked me to cut his hair out on the patio. Even though I informed him that I had only cut someone's hair once in my life, he insisted. While I was cutting his hair, he said to me, "Mickey, I do not think my daughter is the right person for you." I was speechless. I could not believe that he would tell me this just one day before the wedding. I was afraid to ask him why he said that, and I never learned why he made that comment. In time, I realized that Jennifer's father knew his daughter much better than I did.

Jennifer eagerly arranged everything for the wedding. We were married on September 23, 1993, aboard a chartered yacht. It sailed out of Marina del Rey and offered a full bar, a dining area, and a deck area for dancing. We had 70 guests on the ship. After the wedding ceremony, the ship cruised along at 4 knots while everyone enjoyed drinking, dining, and dancing for three hours. After we disembarked, we were picked up by a limousine and taken to a nice hotel. The next day, we departed on a five-day trip to Honolulu. The wedding and the honeymoon costs exceeded $10,000, none of which Jennifer paid. Even though she was an architect, she had no money.

After we were married, I took Jennifer to Japan to meet my parents. My father was easy-going and did not say anything about her. After our divorce, my mother told me that she did not like the way she looked.

Married Life

When I met Jennifer, she was driving a dilapidated old car. After we were married, I purchased a 1986 Isuzu Impulse for her to drive. Not long after that, I leased a new 1994 Camry V6 for her. We opened a joint checking account and pooled our earnings in one account. Since I had been divorced once before, I really wanted this marriage to work. I did not want to repeat the same mistakes. However, it was beginning to dawn on me that she married me for financial reasons.

Even though Jennifer did not make a significant contribution to our joint bank account, she spent an unreasonable amount of money on unnecessary personal items without consulting with me. We got into countless arguments about finances. During one such argument, I gave in and agreed to give her a personal allowance of $600 a month and allot only $400 for my personal spending. I felt that this was the only way I could control her perpetual spending. But I soon learned she continued to spend money on frivolous things. She purchased a hand-held gaming device on which she played the Super Mario Brothers game. In fact, she constantly played the game. It reached the point where it began to interfere with our married life.

I implored her to spend less time playing Super Mario Brothers, but she ignored my pleas. My frustrations escalated. One night, while she was playing the game, I tore the device out of her hands and smashed it to pieces. Despite these setbacks, I still believed we were doing fine as a couple.

Another evening, before she came home from work, the phone rang. I answered it. It was some guy I did not know. He asked for Jennifer and told me they were supposed to go jogging together on Venice Beach. This aroused my suspicions, but I did not say anything about the phone call to her.

Jennifer's True Colors

My daughters arrived in Redondo Beach to spend the Thanksgiving holiday with us. That Friday, we had plans to spend the day at Six Flags Magic Mountain. On Friday morning, Jennifer suddenly claimed that she was too sick to go. This seemed a little strange to me, but I left for the theme park with my daughters anyway.

On Saturday, Jennifer and I sent the girls off at the airport. I did not notice anything strange about her behavior that day. When Monday came, I left for work as usual. After I returned home at 5:30 p.m., I saw that the light in the living room had been left on. This seemed rather strange to me. When I entered the house, I immediately knew something was wrong. Although some items still remained, the room was basically stripped clean. My first thought was that we had been burglarized.

I immediately ran upstairs to check Jennifer's room. We shared the same bed, but she used the second bedroom to store her personal things. My heart sank when I found the room completely empty, and I felt faint. I had never imagined coming home and finding this scene.

I climbed the stairs to our bedroom and found two letters on the bed. One was addressed to me and the other to my daughters. In the letter to me, she basically told me that she had been dreading coming home every day. It became painfully clear that she wanted to spend her married life with me as if she were a single person. I tried to call her sister, but she pretended that she did not know anything about Jennifer's situation or where she had gone.

Jennifer wrongfully took all the gifts we had received from my friends for our wedding. I later learned that she withdrew half of the funds from our joint bank account, which was $8,000. Most of the money was what I had deposited into the account. She apparently used some of that money to put a deposit down for a new apartment somewhere else.

I later checked my phone records and learned that while my daughters and I were at Six Flags Magic Mountain, she contacted numerous apartments near her workplace as well as various movers. So, it became clear that as soon as I left for work on Monday, the mover came in. She had coordinated everything perfectly in a limited amount of time. She also took the Camry that was leased under my name.

I had married a true gold-digger.

Leading up to the Divorce

I had never visited Jennifer at her workplace, but I knew the name of the firm in Venice Beach where she worked. The next morning, I was waiting for her in the company's parking garage. The look on her face after she saw me was priceless. All the blood drained from her face and she looked as though someone were about to kill her.

We sat on a bench at the beach and talked for a while. We agreed that we should seek counseling. The counselor we ultimately ended up working with was very nice, but he was not very effective as a counselor.

One day, Jennifer called me upset and crying. She told me that she had been depressed over the way her eyes and nose looked. She said she wanted to have plastic surgery to improve her appearance. She told me she had already researched the cost of having surgery, but she could not afford it. She begged me to pay for her plastic surgery. She knew how to play with my emotions and she played me well. Out of sympathy, I paid over $8,000.

Even after that, she still wanted more money from me and she hired a lawyer. We had only been married for thirteen months, and I knew that our marriage had been too short for her to collect any money from me. A lot of things had happened before I agreed to a divorce. She returned my Camry and moved to Las Vegas. Jennifer filed for divorce on April 30, 1996.

After our divorce was final, my mother asked me why I had married such an ugly woman. She said her eyes looked like a fox's eyes. Jennifer later confessed that the eye surgery was not a success; she was unable to close her eyes completely. In Las Vegas, she often woke up in the middle of the night because her eyes became dry and she could not sleep.

Sometimes karma catches up with people.

I Should Have Known Better

After the divorce, I resumed my search for a potential mate. I met a lady through the dating service, and after talking to her over the phone, we agreed to meet near her home after Christmas.

I spent the Christmas holiday with my daughters and received a fart machine from them as a gag gift. This machine was capable of producing various sounds associated with flatulence. On the return trip, I was to meet my date near her home and we were going to go to a restaurant to talk.

I should have known better, but my crazy mischievous side got the better part of me. I placed the fart machine under the passenger seat of my car and waited for the right moment. Once both of us were seated in my car, I activated the fart machine to produce the most disgusting fart sound imaginable. The sound took my date by surprise and she looked very embarrassed. She tried to motion to me that the sound did not emanate from her. I immediately confessed that it was me. I tried to explain that the machine was a Christmas gift from my daughters and I simply wanted to check if it really worked. However, the damage was already done. Although we had a pleasant conversation over a meal, she never responded to my phone messages afterwards.

Business Trip to Scotland

In 1995, I was asked by our parent company to go to Scotland and repair an airless degreaser they had sold to a Japanese company there. Before I left, I felt some discomfort in my lumbar area. I arrived at Glasgow

International Airport on December 27, 1995, where I was met by a Japanese employee of the company, Mr. Ohta.

I was wearing a fanny pack around my waist for convenience. I learned that in Scotland, the word *fanny* meant vagina. So, I decided that I would use this knowledge to be funny. As I was checking in at the hotel, a female clerk was assisting me. I thought I would try my joke on her, and I told her that I was carrying a fanny pack because it was convenient. I was hoping that she would interpret that I was carrying a vagina pack because it was convenient. Instead, she appeared to be annoyed and ignored me.

The next day, Mr. Ohta introduced me to the sights and sounds of Scotland, including Edinburgh Castle. For the first time in my life, I ate French fries dipped in vinegar. In the U.S., we normally eat them with ketchup.

That evening, I started feeling sciatica-like pains in my left hip and thigh area, but I worked on repairing the degreaser for two days in great pain. By the time I finished my work, I was limping noticeably.

Pain or No Pain

In an effort to be hospitable, Mr. Ohta suggested that I experience a Scottish prostitute. Even though I was feeling some sciatic pain, I could not pass up his offer.

He took me to a "pleasure house" whose front door was below street level. We climbed down five steps and opened the front door. Inside, we saw seven or eight ladies standing against the walls. There were a small coffee table and a sofa in the room. The place looked like it was once someone's residence. Some of the customers were talking to the ladies seated on the sofa.

Most of the ladies looked attractive, and I chose the one who resembled Morgan Fairchild, a blonde American actress who became popular in the early 1970s. She led me to a spacious, dimly lit room with a round bed. We talked briefly and got down to business. She was prepared and had protection ready for me. During the course of our business, I saw that her arm was covered with warts. I began to worry. What would happen if I caught the virus that plagued her? Due to my sciatic pains, my usual, well-oiled butterfly motion was not very smooth. But somehow, I finished my business and showered there. I came back to my hotel limping badly with pain.

Going Home to Los Angeles

The next day, I was scheduled to depart for Los Angeles. Mr. Ohta accompanied me to the airport. He was worried about my back.

I did not have a direct flight to Los Angeles and had to change planes at Heathrow Airport. For the flight back to Los Angeles, I asked the flight attendant to give me a seat with more leg room due to my pains, which she did.

The trip from Glasgow to Los Angeles lasted fifteen hours, and I was in agony. I had to shift my position in my seat constantly to ease the pain. I was convinced that making love to the prostitute had made my back much worse. As soon as I arrived in Los Angeles, I went to an urgent care facility, where the doctor prescribed a Medrol Dosepak for me. Miraculously, it got rid of the pain in five days.

My Father Passed Away

My father started experiencing problems with his heart in his late fifties. He never drank, but he used to smoke a pack of cigarettes a day. He eventually followed his doctor's advice and quit smoking. When I went back to visit my parents, I took my father's pulse by placing my fingers on his wrist. I knew then that he had really bad arrythmia even though he said he did not feel it. This was unimaginable to me, since I had experienced an irregular heartbeat from time to time and knew that it was clearly noticeable. His heart condition worsened in his early seventies, but we were told that surgery was not an option due to his advanced age. A few months before he passed away, he suffered from an enlarged heart and fluid accumulation in his abdomen.

I received a call from my cousin on January 11, 1995, advising me that my father might not live too long. He urged me to come to Nagano as soon as possible. When I arrived, I learned that my mother had been keeping vigil by his bedside for twenty-four hours a day. I spent the next ten days going back and forth between the hospital and my parents' house. My father's condition seemed to stabilize, and I decided to return to the U.S. on January 24, 1995. Before my cousin dropped me off at the train station, I stopped by the hospital to see my father, which would be the last time. When I saw him, he mustered up his best smile and gave me his watch. I believe he knew that he would not live very long.

One January 31, 1995 (February 1, Japan time), my cousin phoned me and told me that my father had passed away. Immediately after we hung up, I arranged for an airplane ticket and left for Japan the next day to attend the funeral. I felt really bad that I never thanked him for all he had done for me. Without his help, I would not be where I am now. I still feel guilty about it.

My mother later told me that my father did a big favor for her as well. He managed to live long enough to enable her to collect his social security benefits for the month of February.

Day Trader

In 1996, one of my Japanese friends told me that he had started trading stocks online. This was considered the pre-bubble period; an economic bubble is a period when current asset prices greatly exceed their intrinsic valuation.

After my friend gave me a brief lesson in online trading, I opened an account with one of the online trading companies. Initially, I started off with small scale trades, but gradually I became braver and more obsessed. I became a day trader and traded whenever I had time. At the peak of the dot com period, I had over $100,000 in my account and margin.

During a margin call, if you decide to sell your stocks and other securities, you may sell them at substantially lower prices than you paid for them. This is exactly what happened to me when I owned 800 shares of Yahoo stock. In a matter of hours, the stock price plummeted and I received a margin call. As usual, I panicked and sold my entire holdings of Yahoo stock. At the end of the day, I lost $18,000.

As you may know, trading in stocks is somewhat similar to gambling. Historically, I have been a lousy gambler. Even though I thoroughly researched the stocks I wanted to buy, I ultimately lost more money than I made. I clearly was not a well-disciplined stock trader.

The dot com bubble lasted about two years between 1998 and 2000. During that period, I had averaged 450 trades per year; for each transaction, my online trading company charged me a fee of $10. In the end, I paid $4,500 in transactions fees each year. When I filed my federal tax return, I had to make 450 individual entries by hand on the tax form, which took me more than four hours to complete.

I still maintain an investment account and invest in big name companies such as Google, Amazon, Apple, Microsoft, Tesla, and Nvidia. But I seldom trade nowadays. I think I have learned my lessons the hard way.

The Search for a Girlfriend Widens

My experiences with the dating service were less than stellar, so I decided to widen my search. A friend of mine happened to mention that her friends from Brazil had recently visited Florida and had a good time there. I asked her if she could introduce me to a young Brazilian girl, and she did. She gave me the address of one of the girls who had visited Florida.

Immediately, I embarked on the task of learning Portuguese. I purchased a Portuguese language book with a cassette learning tape. Since I had taken one semester of Spanish at a local junior college, learning Portuguese was not that difficult. Also, my brain was not as foggy as it is now.

I wrote to the young woman in Portuguese and asked her if she would be interested in getting to know me. I also enclosed a photo in my letter. Within two weeks, I received her response and her photo.

Valeria was twenty-nine and I was forty-four years old at the time. She provided her fax number, and we began to communicate regularly through fax. She was surprised by how well I could write in Portuguese. One day, I decided to call her on the telephone. We talked, but I found that it was very difficult to communicate with her verbally. Still, I was not discouraged and looked forward to getting to know her better.

After three months of exchanging letters, we agreed to meet in Belém, Brazil, where she lived. Belém is the capital city of Pará, a state located in northern Brazil. It is both a port city and the gateway to Brazil's lower Amazon region. Due to the vast number of mango trees throughout the city, it is also known as *Cidade das Mangueiras* (City of Mango Trees).

I took two weeks of vacation from work and departed for Belém on November 3, 1996. Before I left for Brazil, I went shopping for gifts for Valeria and her parents and found a nice bottle of perfume for her. I told her that I would be arriving at Belém/Val-de-Cans Júlio Cezar Ribeiro International Airport at 6 a.m. on November 4. There were no direct flights to Belém, so I had to board a connecting flight in Miami. It was a long journey to Brazil from Los Angeles.

When I arrived, I expected her to meet me at the airport, but she was nowhere to be seen. I was really shocked by this and sat on a chair at the airport for thirty minutes waiting for her. I must have looked very dejected because people around me took notice and asked me what was wrong.

One gentleman was kind enough to pick up the phone to call Valeria for me. He told her that I was at the airport waiting for her to pick me up. She gave him the dubious excuse that she had overslept. This was not a good start.

Thirty minutes later, Valeria showed up at the airport. I was not in a good mood, but I tried to be as cheerful as I could. She did not look at all like what I had expected. She told me that she had borrowed her sister's small BMW. I thought she did this to try to impress me.

We left the airport, and almost immediately I found myself in a very squalid area of town. In all my life, I had never seen a slum like this one. In fact, I could not have imagined such a ghetto in my wildest dreams. Countless young people were just sitting out in the streets doing absolutely nothing. The roads were unpaved and dusty.

While we were driving, Valeria played a cassette tape featuring a male opera singer whom I had not heard of. She appeared to be enjoying the music and asked me if I liked opera. Since I was not a good liar, I told her no, which I think turned her off.

We finally arrived at her parents' house in a gated community. Upon being introduced to everyone in her household, I gave them the gifts I had purchased for them. They seemed overjoyed to receive them. I was surprised that they had a maid. I was told that even a household with an average income had a maid at their service. Valeria's father owned a fruit distribution business. Although she worked there, I thought she was spoiled.

Later that day, Valeria, her father, and her 12-year-old brother took me to the only shopping mall in town. I believe this was another attempt to try to impress me. Although the mall was large, nothing in this town impressed me.

Afterward, she drove me to my hotel, where we enjoyed a nice dinner in the hotel restaurant. The following day, she did not get in touch with me. I spent most of my time reading the newspaper and watching TV.

On the third day, she took me to her sister's apartment. They also had a maid. We all boarded their Volkswagen bus and drove to their fruit orchards by the Amazon River. When we returned, Valeria's sister and brother-in-law welcomed me with a big barbeque party. I had a feeling that they sensed Valeria was not treating me properly, although I came all the way from the U.S. to see her. They genuinely did everything they could to make me feel welcome. At one point, Valeria's brother asked me why I came all the way to see her; it appeared he really liked me.

The next day, I met Valeria at a restaurant near my hotel to talk about our future together. We both agreed that this relationship was not worth pursuing. The following day, I walked two miles to a travel agency in downtown Belém and changed my flight to an earlier one. Valeria drove me to the airport in her sister's car. I gave her a letter addressed to her sister and her husband. I wanted to let them know how grateful I was to have had an opportunity to meet them.

Gambling Fever Rekindled

One of the reasons why I decided to move from San Luis Obispo was to put distance between myself and my frequent gambling destinations.

Lake Tahoe was 400 miles away from SLO and Reno was 430 miles away. Moving to Los Angeles changed all of that. I now live a mere 287 miles away from Sin City (Las Vegas). Although temptation is not a sin, giving in to temptation is. Living much closer to the city of temptation rekindled my gambling fever.

Starting in 1997, I traveled to Las Vegas alone every two months to play blackjack. This addiction lasted for the next two to three years. I was earning substantially more than I had in San Luis Obispo, and I tended to lose a lot more this time around. Sometimes, I lost more than $2,000 on a visit. When I lost big, I withdrew cash from my VISA card. Fortunately, I was able to pay off the credit card balance within a month and never incurred any interest on the money I had borrowed.

I never stayed at a hotel in Las Vegas, no matter how long I played blackjack or how tired I was. I usually played at the blackjack table for ten to twelve hours straight, without eating, after driving for six hours to get there. When it was over, I just drove back home.

I managed to lose $6,000 each year for the next two years. After that, I just quit going to Las Vegas. It wasn't because I lost the money. It was because I was running out of stamina. The way I gambled required a lot of stamina, and I reached a point where my stamina tank was almost empty.

My Mother Taught Me to Save

I may seem like a financially reckless person after losing so much money gambling and trading stocks, but my mother did teach me to save. She had gone through financially difficult times when she was growing up, and she did not want me to experience what she had experienced. Her father had recklessly invested in commodities and antiques, and that launched his family into destitution.

To achieve financial stability, I began contributing to an IRA and other retirement funds in 1986, and I purchased a townhouse the following year. If I had invested money wisely instead of gambling — and losing heaps of money trading stocks — I would have been much better off financially.

Paying the Price

Scottish writer Jane Welsh Carlyle once said, "The longer I live, the more I am certain that men, in all that relates to their own health, have no common sense!" This is very true. I have done some very reckless things in my life, including competing in aerobics classes with girls half my age. In 1998, living without any regard to my physical strength finally caught up with me.

One day, when I was eating ramen at a Japanese restaurant, I felt a sudden sharp jolt of pain running through my back. Soon afterward, I felt considerable pain and numbness in my left backside. The pain was so intense that I immediately secured an appointment with an orthopedic surgeon. After examining me, he suspected that I had ruptured a disc and ordered an MRI of my lumbar region.

After the MRI session concluded, the technician told me that she had seen an enormous disc rupture in my lumbar, which technicians were not supposed to tell their patients. The day after the MRI session, I could barely walk.

When I met with my doctor again the next day, he scheduled the surgery for two days later. Before I left his office, I asked his assistant about the doctor's past surgical track record. He responded, "Excellent!" I was relieved to hear that.

Prior to going into surgery, I asked the doctor how he knew he was operating on the right disc. He assured me that he was using an x-ray marker to pinpoint the correct disc on which to operate. I also asked him to preserve whatever he removed from my disc so that I could take it home. Although my request seemed crazy, I was just curious. He told me he would do his best to accommodate my request, and he did. He placed the material he scraped from my disc on a piece of gauze, took a picture of it, and gave to me.

Minimally invasive surgeries are common these days, but mine was a traditional open surgery that required a substantially longer recuperation time. When the anesthesia wore off, I woke up in a hospital bed. When my doctor came in to check me the next morning, I was still in great pain. He assured me that the pain would subside soon, and I was discharged the same day.

He Operated on the Wrong Disc

Two days after being discharged, I was still in considerable pain and went back to see my surgeon. He ordered another MRI at a different facility. After the session was over, the radiologist approached me and asked me if I had had lumbar surgery recently. After hearing my response, she told me that I might have cancer in my lumbar area. Twice, in two separate facilities, the medical staff acted unethically. Her comment really shocked and worried me.

The next day, I saw my doctor again. Upon examining the MRI images and reviewing the corresponding report, he admitted that he had operated on the wrong disc. Instead of L5 and S1, he had operated on L4 and L5. I was in excruciating pain and had no choice but to ask him to operate again to correct his mistake. Later on, after hearing my story, a lot of people asked me why I trusted him to perform surgery on me a second time.

After the second surgery, I was lying in my hospital bed at night and felt the sudden need to relieve myself. I tried unsuccessfully to lower the metal guard on my hospital bed so I could get up and go to the bathroom. In desperation, I jumped over it instead. I was still woozy after the anesthesia and could not accomplish what I had to do. I jumped back in bed and summoned a nurse to catheterize me. The next morning, I did not want to suffer the humiliation of having the nurse remove the catheter, so I attempted to remove it myself. After struggling in vain for a few minutes, I called the nurse and asked her to remove it. She explained to me that the catheter had a mechanism to prevent patients from removing it by themselves. I was discharged the same day.

I do not recall if I attended rehabilitation sessions for my back. Ten days after the surgery, I returned to the gym and started pumping iron again. Two years after having the surgery, someone told me that I was walking like an orangutan, which really shocked and embarrassed me. It took years to fully recover from the surgery.

Time to Sue the Surgeon

Although the surgeon paid all of my medical expenses and compensated me for my time lost from work, I was not going to let him off the hook that easily. Under the law, I was eligible to collect a maximum amount of $250,000. I hired a lawyer.

The judge suggested that we settle the case through mediation rather than going to court, and a mediator was appointed. The mediation meeting took place in my attorney's office without me being present.

As I waited, my lawyer kept coming in and out of the meeting to tell me the settlement the insurance company was willing to offer. When it was over, I hesitantly agreed on a settlement of $100,000. One third of the settlement was paid to my lawyer for his services, and I received a little over $66,000. In hindsight, I should have gone to court to get more money, but I really wanted to get my hands on the cash as soon as possible so I could invest that money in stocks. I thought I could double or triple the money, and the pain and agony that I had endured would be forgotten. True to form, I lost the entire amount in just three months.

Christmas Tree Trimming

I purchased a two-foot potted Christmas tree in 1991. When the holidays were over, I did not want to throw the tree into the dumpster. Instead, I planted it in the corner of my patio.

In seven years, the unexpected happened. The tree grew in height from two feet to eighteen feet and the diameter of its trunk reached twelve inches. Naturally, my neighbors began to complain, and I knew I had to do something about it. I did not want to hire someone to come trim the tree, so I decided to do it myself, even though I had had back surgeries only two months earlier.

When my neighbors found out, they said I was crazy. But when I am determined to do something, nothing will stop me. Fortunately, I finished trimming the tree without any major incidents or suffering any ill effects on my surgically repaired back.

1998 Nagano Winter Olympics

Three years before the historic 1998 Nagano Winter Olympics were scheduled to take place, I took my younger daughter, Lynn, to Nagano to see my parents.

At that time, the main stadium was still under construction just a quarter of a mile away from my parents' house. Hosting the Olympics was very beneficial for Nagano. It resulted in the building of many new roads and the launch of the Hokuriku Shinkansen (bullet train). The bullet train connected Nagano with Tokyo, enabling travel between the two cities in just eighty-two minutes. Lynn and I took many walks together and inspected the various structures and buildings being constructed for the Olympics.

During the Olympics, the foreign broadcasters managed to get on the nerves of Nagano citizens and Japanese people in general, by mispronouncing Nagano. They emphasized the "Na" in Nagano when there should have been no emphasis at all. It is simply [naga⁺no].

Visiting My Mother

In 2000, several life insurance policies my mother had taken out in my name matured, and she wanted to give that money to me. My mother was a very frugal individual, and she worked hard all her life, saving money and spending very little of it on herself.

She was a diminutive woman, merely 4'10" tall and weighing only 80 pounds. Yet, at the age of 77, she was still working in her apple and peach orchards for twelve hours a day, sometimes lifting boxes of fruit weighing as much as sixty pounds. The fruits she grew commanded a good price at the market, and she was able to save a substantial amount of money over time. She said she did not need the money from the life insurance policies, so we went to the bank together and transferred those funds into my bank account in the United States.

I did not lose that money in gambling or risky stock investments.

She retired at age 88, and I wanted to take her to a nice *onsen* (hot spring resort), but she adamantly turned me down. She stubbornly insisted that I should not spend any money on her.

Shoulder Surgery

I did not learn my lesson from my back surgeries and continued to push myself at the gym beyond what my body could physically handle. In time, I tore my labrum and rotator cuff, requiring surgery. My trusted surgeon, Dr. Borden (not the same doctor who performed my back surgeries) repaired my shoulder laparoscopically. My rebab began the very next day, when I could barely lift a one-pound dumbbell.

It took me almost nine months to fully recover from this injury. Even at age 71, I still think that I can push myself physically despite my body letting me know otherwise.

Having Fun with Ponta

In 2002, I received a call from one of my friends from San Luis Obispo who was living in Japan. He told me that customs officials at Los Angeles International Airport confiscated $10,000 from a friend when the friend failed to disclose it. I nicknamed this man Ponta, because in Japanese the name implies that the individual is somewhat senseless and does senseless things.

Ponta owned a small antique shop in Saitama, Japan and traveled to Los Angeles every two months to purchase the vintage jeans and Air Jordan shoes he sold in his shop. At this time, these particular goods commanded really good prices in Japan.

My friend asked me to help Ponta recover his money from customs. He told me that Ponta was in his mid-thirties, and he would be calling me. As anticipated, he called me, and I immediately called him Ponta. I don't know if the name offended him. He did not seem to object to being called Ponta. He explained the situation to me in detail, and we agreed to meet at my townhouse that evening.

Ponta Arrives

My long dormant mischievousness suddenly awakened, and I was determined to have a lot of fun with this guy since I had the upper hand in the situation. Just before he arrived, I concealed myself behind a three-foot tall bush planted in the corner of my patio fence by the front door. The area was dimly lit, and I quietly lay in wait.

As he walked past the bush, I told myself, "Here he comes!" I jumped out of the bush with both hands up in the air and screamed, "Waaa!" He was startled and immediately fell to the ground. He looked as though he was about to be mugged. He told me that I had scared him to death since we were total strangers to one another, and he was uncertain if he had come to the right place.

I told him that I was mischievous in nature, and I might do it to him again. I promised him that I would check with customs regarding how to retrieve his confiscated money.

Ponta Returns

Ponta returned to Japan. Nearly two months later, he sent me an email informing me of his impending travel to Los Angeles to buy more jeans and shoes. He wanted to see me again, so we set a time, date, and place to meet. He told me that he wanted to treat me to dinner to show his appreciation for the help I had given to him.

We were to meet at my townhouse again in the evening. Needless to say, I was excited to have fun with him again. This time, in the dark, I scaled six feet up a tree and waited for his arrival. As he approached, I jumped from the tree and onto his back. We both fell to the ground, and fortunately neither of us were hurt. He simply could not believe that someone would do the things that I had done to him. I told him that he had been forewarned.

He could not get rid of me even if he wanted to, because customs had indicated that it would take another eight months for them to process his application to retrieve his money.

Ponta's Wife

Ponta being a ponta, he made the mistake of telling me that his wife began calling him by that name after she heard what I had done to him. In fact, she was looking forward to learning what I would do next. I certainly did not need any encouragement, but I felt further motivated knowing that she was behind me.

Ponta and I were scheduled to meet again at my townhouse at noon. I was certain that by this time he would be very careful to ensure that I would not jump out at him. He reached the front door and knocked. I was in the second-floor bathroom and saw him standing there through the bathroom window. Anticipating his arrival, I had already prepared a small bucket full of water. I grabbed the bucket by its handle and dumped its contents out the bathroom window. In less than a second, I heard him scream an expletive in Japanese. This time, I treated him to lunch.

Meeting Ponta in Japan

One month after the last incident, I traveled to Japan. I suggested that Ponta meet me at the Shinjuku train station in the morning. I am fairly certain that Ponta was confident that I would not pull a prank on him at a crowded train station. He was mistaken.

I spotted him in the crowd and crept up behind him without him knowing. As he was searching for me in the crowd, I sprung up on his back and yelled, "Waaaa!" We both fell to the ground as the crowd around us looked shocked and confused. I told them it was just a prank and we walked away.

We had lunch together afterwards, and Ponta confessed that he had been embarrassed by what I did to him in public. I told him that his embarrassment gave me joy.

Ponta's Landing Technique

Ponta and I were to meet in Hermosa Beach, California, and have dinner together. I went to his motel and called him to let him know that I was waiting for him downstairs. Before he came downstairs, I snuck behind the building and waited for him. He came down and walked over to the sidewalk, where he began searching for me.

Just like at the Shinjuku Station, I jumped on his back. This time, I was surprised that he did not fall to the ground as before. Ponta had finally mastered the perfect landing technique.

I clearly took advantage of the situation and abused him, knowing that he could not afford to get angry at me. Without my help, he would never be able to retrieve his $10,000 from customs.

Ponta Gets his Money Back

Ponta was fortunate that customs released his money earlier than we had expected and sent the check bearing his name to me. On his subsequent visit to Los Angeles, we decided to meet at my townhouse and go to a Japanese restaurant with the promise that I would not do anything to him.

However, during his last two visits, I kept mentioning to him that it would be funny if I smeared excrement on his door handle. I had adequately brainwashed him with this talk. While we were in the restaurant waiting for our meals to be served, I excused myself to go to my car to get something. I brought a tube of toothpaste with me and smeared some of it under the passenger's side door handle of my car, in a manner in which he could not see it.

He was elated after I gave him the check I received from customs, and he clearly was not thinking about being pranked. We finished eating and we went outside to my car. As soon as he tried to open the passenger side door, he screamed an expletive in Japanese. He said, "You promised that you would not do this again!" In hindsight, I should have used peanut butter as it would have made a stronger impact.

That was the last time I saw Ponta or heard from him again. I had a great deal of fun at his expense, for which I am grateful.

The New Toy

In 2003, I treated myself to a 2004 Nissan 350Z. I leased the new 1995 Toyota Camry for my second wife, so the Nissan was the first car I purchased new with cash. All my previous cars were purchased using cash, but they were all used vehicles.

xx. My 2004 Nissan 350Z

I loved the smell of the new car, and it was just beautiful. It was painted a flashy, metallic blue. The car was very eye-catching, but I wanted to make it stick out in the crowd even more. Putting my well-honed skills to use, I installed a whale tale, red and white decals on the sides and the hood, a set of 20-inch wheels with a set of low-profile tires, a free flow air cleaner, an intake manifold spacer, front camber kits, rear adjustable stabilizer bars, springs to lower the car, and a car bra. With these upgrades, it was difficult not to notice the car. A lot of people complimented me on it. The added benefit was that the car really cornered well with these modifications.

I enjoyed owning the vehicle for ten years; it was an incredibly long time for me to own the same car. I simply used the car for transportation, and I never used it for autocross.

The Merger

Since 1988, I had been steadily employed by the Japanese company and mainly sold airless degreasers. However, our former competitor wanted desperately to merge with our company. In 2003, the merger was formalized and a new company, headquartered in Rhode Island, was established. The Torrance facility was sold, and a new location serving as the West Coast office was established in Lomita, about three miles from our original facility.

When the new company was established, I was forced to invest $10,000 of my own money in it. I was given the title of vice president, but I worked alone from our new office in Lomita. The new company consisted of only seven employees including me.

In the beginning we did well, but I eventually realized that there was no future for me there. I resigned from the company in October 2008.

An American Citizen

When 2006 rolled around, there were rumors that some of the privileges I enjoyed as a green card holder would no longer be available. I did not want to take a chance and decided to obtain American citizenship. One of the benefits of citizenship is the ability to change your name. I considered changing my name from Masayuki to Mickey, but I did not follow through with it. I even thought about changing it to José Gonzales, just to be funny.

Around this time, I was in the habit of using the name José Gonzales on restaurant waiting lists. I took pleasure from seeing the strange looks on people's faces when I stood up after that name was called. I do not look remotely Mexican.

I attended the swearing-in ceremony with a few thousand people who had also recently obtained their citizenship.

F1 Service Company

After I resigned in 2008, I established my own company called F1 Service Company. My company's name is derived from the airless degreasers I sold, which were called F1 Clean. I am the sole proprietor and work out of my home office. After fifteen years in business, I believe this is the best decision I have ever made.

F1 Service Company's primary functions include selling and servicing the airless degreasers manufactured by the old company in Japan. I also sell service parts for the existing airless degreasers. My company has no financial ties to the old company in Japan. We are strictly business associates.

My company has functioned in the same manner since I first established it fifteen years ago. I sold plenty of airless degreasers while I was employed with the old companies, and I have enough service calls and parts sales to sustain an annual income close to six figures. Occasionally,

I sell an airless degreaser and make a good profit. I have established set rates for service calls and travel time.

The bottom line is that I really enjoy fixing these machines. As I work on the airless degreasers, I feel as though I am getting paid good money to enjoy a hobby. Sometimes, I try to help my customers fix their problems over the phone free of charge.

I make my own hours, and I am my own boss. Essentially, I work an average of less than two hours per day whenever I feel like it. This truly is the best job that I have ever had.

My Third Wife

I was a member of an online dating service called Match.com. One day in 2007, I received a notification that I had been selected by one of their members. When I checked her profile, I was pleasantly surprised to find that she was very cute and young. Her blond hair was a plus; my previous two wives were also blond.

She grew up in Chicago and graduated from DePaul University. She worked for one of the big accounting firms in Los Angeles.

I called her, and we talked for a while. We seemed to be compatible, as she was interested in Japanese culture and men. We set up a date for that weekend.

Our First Date

I was able to infer from our conversation that Kris was the type of person who would appreciate my funny side. On our first date, we had arranged to see a movie and have dinner at a nearby Mexican restaurant. We had agreed to drive our separate cars and meet at the theater.

When I arrived, I saw her sitting on a bench in front of some shrubs not far from the theater. My mischievous side took over and I decided to surprise her from behind. I walked through the shrubs and snuck up behind her without her noticing me. Then, from behind her left shoulder, I poked my face out and said, "Hello!" She looked surprised at first but took it all in stride. Who would have thought that someone you barely knew would act this way?

We stopped in at an ice cream shop before the movie started, and the rest of the date went smoothly. We agreed to meet again.

Kris Moved into My Townhouse

After dating for three months, I asked Kris to move in with me. I posed the question to her at the hospital while she was sitting by my bedside in the emergency room. She had driven me to the hospital after I suffered a nasty episode with kidney stones.

She agreed, and in June 2007, we hired movers and moved all of her belongings into my townhouse. Before she moved in, my place was very plain, yet functional. With her feminine touch and flare for interior decorating, she transformed my place into a very nice place to live.

Since my townhouse is only one mile from the beach, we went there on weekends and enjoyed walking together on The Strand. We went to a movie once a week, and she was always finding fun things for us to do such as visiting museums, going to live concerts, car shows, and Japanese gardens. We also took numerous trips together including a cruise to Mexico, vacations in Las Vegas, Hawaii, and many other places.

My travels to Vegas with Kris were not as financially devastating as they were in the past. She knew about my past gambling habit and forced me to leave the blackjack table when she thought it was time. As a matter of priority, I obliged. We have gone to Las Vegas several times, and I have lost less than $100.

Kris loves to travel, and Hawaii and Japan are among our favorite places to visit. Since visiting Oahu on our honeymoon, we have traveled there three more times. We have seen and done just about all there is to do in Oahu with the exception of surfing and snorkeling, since Kris is not too fond of the water.

We have traveled to Japan four times since 2008, and I am happy to say that we did not spend a penny on airfare. Our credit cards enable us to earn airline miles. It is particularly easy for me to accumulate mileage with my business purchases, and we usually take full advantage of it.

Unfortunately, our travels halted when the COVID-19 pandemic began. I am currently sitting on over 400,000 airline miles, which I hope to use next year when we visit Japan again.

xxi. Ueno Park, Japan

Our First Trip Together to Japan

We traveled to Japan for the first time together in 2008 to see my mother and do some sightseeing in Nagano and Tokyo. Since Ponta had been so embarrassed by my antics in public, it was time to see how Kris would react.

While we were strolling through a small park near the Ueno train station, I spotted an interesting water fountain where the water was streaming into the pond in a semi-arch shape. Standing at the side of the fountain, I had an idea for an interesting photo. With Kris' guidance, I managed to position myself to the left of the origin of the stream, where I posed to resemble the bronze fountain sculpture in central Brussels known as *Manneken Pis* (Dutch for "Little Pissing Man"). Just at the right moment, she snapped a couple of memorable photos. There were a lot of people around us, but Kris did not care. Her priority was to capture this memorable moment with her camera.

Needless to say, she passed the test. She does not get embarrassed easily when I act crazily in public. We did the same thing when we visited Balboa Park in San Diego a few years later.

Memorable Los Angeles Clippers Game

I have been an avid Clippers fan since 1986. Having grown up in Chicago, Kris was a Bulls fan, but she became an avid Clippers fan after she met me. Today, we both love the same sports teams, the Los Angeles Clippers and the Los Angeles Angels.

In 2008, we had tickets for the Clippers game. In the past, we had attended games where a few lucky people seated in the cheap seats were upgraded to premium courtside seats. We wanted to get upgraded, too. I purchased two $15 tickets for seats located in section 300. We purchased a white cotton pillowcase, unstitched it, and made a banner using red, blue, and black markers. We decorated the banner with the Clipper's logo and various other things.

On game day, we arrived at the Staples Center (currently called Crypto.com Arena) forty minutes before the game. As people began filling the stadium, we unfurled our banner and shouted at the top of our lungs, "Clipper Nation, we love you! Go Clippers!" Sure enough, one staff member approached us and asked us to follow him. He led us to courtside seats and handed us two tickets valued at $550 each. Kris and I were ecstatic and winked at each other. Our investment had paid off. They interviewed us during half time, which helped make the day even more memorable for us.

A similar act contributed to us getting upgraded the following year. A few years later, as I was returning from a bathroom break, I was stopped and interviewed by a television crew. Afterwards, the crew awarded me with an official NBA Clippers long sleeve shirt. All in all, we have received tickets and merchandise worth over $2,000 from the Clipper's franchise over the years. We still attend numerous Clippers and Angels games every year.

Helicopter Welcome

Since meeting Kris, I have surprised her with several well-thought-out acts of silliness. While she was away at work, I went to a Big 5 store and purchased a small, radio-controlled helicopter. I brought it home and practiced flying it indoors until I mastered the techniques. I made a small banner with the words, "I love you!" written on it and attached it to one of the helicopter's skids. I also attached a small, red rose.

When I heard the garage door open and close, I knew that Kris had come home. I picked up the remote control and the helicopter took flight. When Kris opened the door to the living room, she was greeted by the helicopter flying the banner I had made and the small, red rose I had picked from our garden. She was surprised at first, but she did enjoy my welcoming her back this way. She later commented that she heard a buzzing sound as she ascended the stairs and did not know what was happening. Living with me, one must expect the unexpected.

Sumo Wrestler Welcome

I surprised Kris yet again when she came home from work. This time, I purchased an inflatable sumo wrestler costume from Amazon. When I put it on and inflated it, I thought it looked interesting, but something was missing. I came up with an idea to make the costume more appealing.

I went to a neighborhood Dollar Tree store, where I purchased a pair of one-inch gold disco balls and a pink Styrofoam cylinder. When I got home, I set about styling a male appendage from these items. The gold disco balls were significant as Kris is familiar with Japanese culture, and she knows that the Japanese slang for testicles is *kintama* (golden balls). After I finished constructing the appendage, I attached it to the sumo wrestler costume with glue. I put the costume on to see how it looked. What I saw in the mirror was a huge sumo wrestler with a disproportionately small appendage, but I liked the overall look. I kept the costume on and waited patiently for Kris to arrive home.

After ten minutes had passed, I began to sweat inside the costume. It was summer, and no air circulated inside the inflatable costume. Fortunately, I heard Kris open and close the garage door. As I listened to her footsteps on the stairs, I could not contain my excitement. As soon as she opened the door and saw me, she screamed and burst into laughter. When she looked at the appendage I had constructed, she commented on my artistic ability; she was impressed with its realistic appearance.

Chippendale Welcome

At this point, Kris really did not know what she would encounter when she returned home from work. I wanted to keep the anticipation and excitement going.

My hair was short and well-groomed at the time. I undressed, put a black bow tie around my neck, and wore a black G-string. The G-string had a mouse face in the front. I stretched out in a provocative pose on the couch and waited for her to come home. When she entered the living room, she screamed and burst into laughter again. It was another successful homecoming.

Kris' Birthday

By now, Kris was fairly used to my antics, but I wanted to surprise her for her birthday. I purchased a long, shiny, platinum blond wig from the Party Store. I also bought a bright red feather boa and a gold "HAPPY BIRTHDAY" cake topper.

I borrowed Kris' makeup and applied eye shadow on my eyelids and bright red lipstick on my lips. I donned the blond wig and fully undressed for this occasion. I had purchased a birthday card for Kris earlier, and I propped it up on top of the coffee table in the living room. Instead of a birthday cake, I found a bright red adult toy and placed the gold "happy birthday" cake topper on top of it, along with a blue and white birthday candle. I wanted to capture the moment for posterity, so I positioned my cellphone on the coffee table and set the photo timer. I reclined on the sofa with the red boa strategically placed to cover my embarrassment. After snapping several sexy photos, I waited for Kris to come home.

She opened the door and found me lying in wait. She screamed in utter disbelief and was overcome with laughter. She never expected to be celebrating her birthday in this fashion.

A Christmas Gift for Kris

I was thinking about giving Kris a unique Christmas present when I happened to see a pair of slippers made from Always maxi pads online. They seemed relatively easy to make and I embarked on making a pair just for her.

xxii. Kris's Christmas slippers

I stole the sanitary pads that she kept in her bathroom cabinet and used a stapler to construct two slippers in just ten minutes. I decorated the tops with tiny red and green metallic gift bows and set them aside to present them to her a few days before Christmas.

Again, before she arrived from work, I placed my handmade slippers on the living room floor in front of the door. I included a handwritten note with them, which read:

> *"Kris, from now on, please wear the slippers provided.*
>
> *Mickey"*

When she came in through the door, she could not miss the surprise that awaited her. Puzzled yet amused, she tried them on. They fit her feet perfectly. Since they were not practical to wear every day, she stashed them away in her closet in a nice box.

Afterwards, I really wanted to try making something that was more complicated and elaborate using maxi pads. I believed she needed something to match her slippers. Since it was getting cold outside, I decided to design a vest for her.

The vest would require more maxi pads than the slippers did, so stealing her maxi pads was not a viable option. I went to the supermarket and purchased a 36-count package of Always maxi pads. I cut the pattern for the vest from a thin sheet of nylon and affixed the pads individually onto the sheet by peeling the protective strips from the adhesive on the back of the pads. I trimmed some sections with a pair of scissors to get them to fit the vest pattern perfectly. After all the maxi pads were attached, I applied clear shipping tape over them to further secure them to the vest. I made

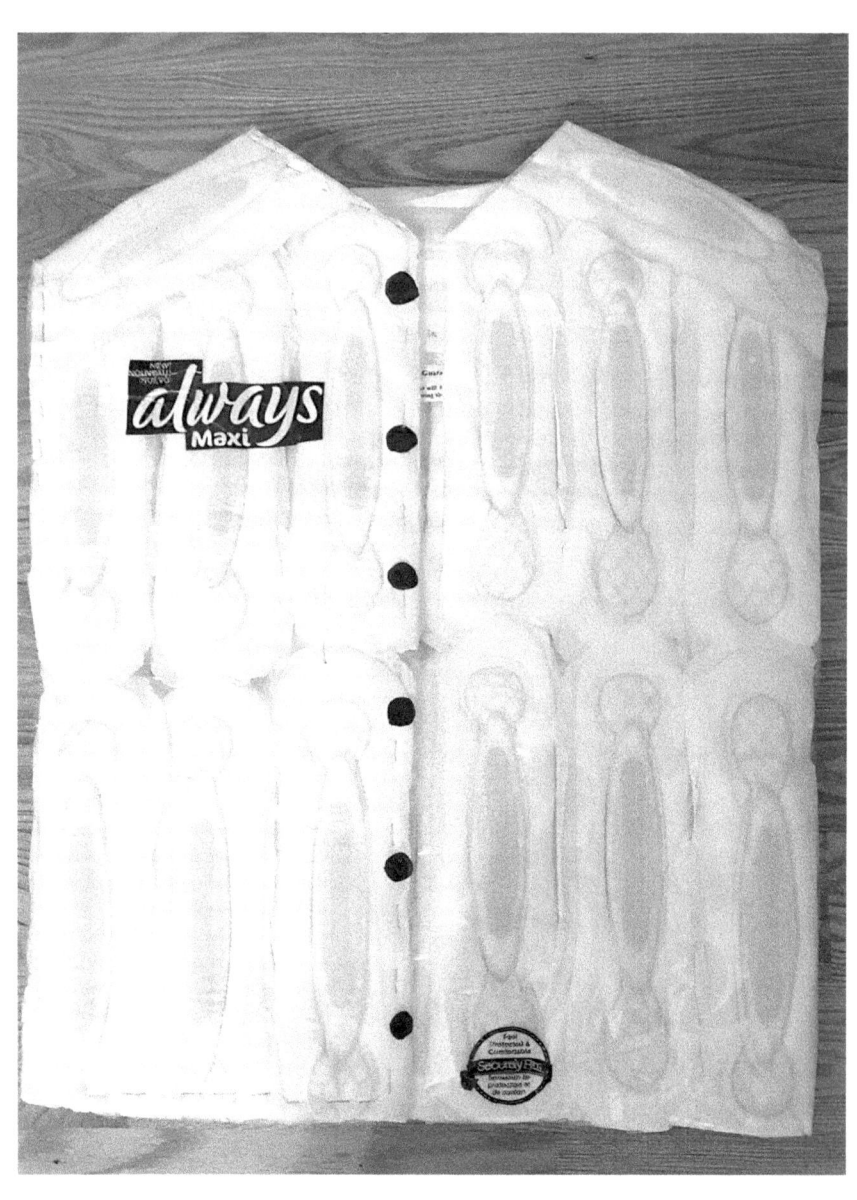

xxiii. The matching vest

sure that the "Always" logo from the package was visible on the right chest area of the vest. I cut out the words, "Feel Protected & Comfortable – Fits Securely" from the package and attached them to the bottom of the vest.

I was satisfied with my creation and waited eagerly for Christmas Day to arrive. When she opened her present, she was bewildered and could not believe the lengths I went through to come up with a unique Christmas gift for her. She reacted to this as she reacted to my earlier antics, by bursting into laughter. The vest fit her snuggly, but she has never worn it in public. It has been hanging on a hanger in her closet ever since. Making that vest was the best three hours I have spent coming up with a way to surprise and amuse Kris.

Shopping at the Supermarket

It would be hard to imagine that anyone would take a mundane act such as shopping at the supermarket and turn it into a comedic adventure. But the fact that Kris takes my mischievous and crazy behavior in stride encourages me to take advantage of any and every opportunity to have some fun.

One of the most annoying things about shopping at the supermarket is being greeted by cashiers in a superficial manner. Often, they ask, "How are you?' without really caring about whether and how you respond to them. It is the same thing when you visit a doctor's office. The receptionist always asks, "How are you?" Do they think I would be visiting a doctor if I were feeling fine? I think a more suitable question in that instance would be, "Hello, what brought you here to see the doctor today?"

So, upon hearing the same superficial question at the supermarket over and over again, I decided to respond, "No good!" This usually breaks them out of their trance and prompts them to ask me why I am not feeling good. Some simply ask why and I tell them to ask my wife. This works out particularly well when Kris is with me as she plays along. The cashier will turn to Kris, and she will respond by saying something like, "He's no good!" or "He's always up to no good!", which really takes the cashier by surprise. Their facial expressions are usually priceless, and we both get a kick out of it.

Kris is also good at keeping a serious face during my supermarket antics. One day, we went to the supermarket together and I had a lollypop in my mouth. I finished eating it while we were shopping and did not know what to do with the white paper stick left over. While we were waiting in the checkout line, I bent the stick into a U-shape and inserted it into my nostrils like the nose ring for cattle. Kris did not say anything and acted completely normal. When we approached the cashier, we did not alter our behavior in any way, and the cashier did not know what to say to us. I am certain that she saw the paper stick in my nose.

Left-Handed Chopsticks

Before the COVID-19 pandemic, Kris and I ate at Japanese restaurants every weekend. I am ambidextrous and can use chopsticks with both hands. I sometimes hold a pair of chopsticks in each hand while I eat, in an effort to be funny and efficient. I normally use my left hand for detail-oriented tasks and my right hand for throwing and writing. I was not ambidextrous by nature, but I trained myself to be that way to be more efficient.

At one particular Japanese restaurant, I normally eat with my right hand. One day, one of our favorite waitresses came to take our order, and I asked her for a pair of left-handed chopsticks. After a brief pause accompanied by a quizzical look on her face, she said, "We do not carry left-handed chopsticks, and I do not think such things exist." That comment really motivated me to come up with a pair of left-handed chopsticks to prove her wrong during our next visit.

I obtained a pair of disposable chopsticks. Disposable chopsticks are typically half-split; the two halves of the chopstick pair are only half separated, and they have to be snapped apart prior to use. Without snapping them apart, I bent them 30 degrees to the left (or to the right depending on how you look at them).

The following weekend, Kris and I went to the same restaurant and I showed our favorite waitress what the left-handed chopsticks looked like. She was quite amazed and said, "I cannot believe that you went through all that trouble just to show me that left-handed chopsticks exist."

The following weekend, we went to a different Japanese restaurant and I asked a young Japanese waiter for a pair of left-handed chopsticks. He was bewildered and did not know what to say. I calmly allowed a few seconds to pass by before telling him, "Do not worry. I brought my own." I pulled out my handmade, curved chopsticks and watched his facial expression change; it was priceless.

I like toying with the waitstaff at restaurants. Oftentimes, when I am asked what I would like to order, I respond by asking the server what the worst item on the menu is. I enjoy the reactions I elicit. My outlandish behavior in public does not bother or embarrass Kris. In fact, I think she actually enjoys it as much as I do. We are very much alike in that regard; we both enjoy watching other people's reactions. One amusing aspect of dining at Japanese restaurants with Kris is that she almost exclusively uses chopsticks while I prefer a fork.

Kris is a highly intelligent person with a sense of humor to match. She has authored eight books, about which you can learn more by visiting her author's website: https://kristineohkubo.wixsite.com/non-fiction-author.

Shirakaba Resort Hotel in Nagano

After my father passed away, whenever I visited my mother in Japan, I tried to take her to a nice *onsen* (hot spring), but she kept refusing because she did not want me to spend the money. Finally, in 2010, Kris and I convinced her to go with us on a two-day trip to a nice resort hotel by the lake. Shirakaba Ikenotaira Hotel is a nice onsen resort located along Lake Shirakaba in Nagano Prefecture. It has both indoor and outdoor co-ed hot spring bathing facilities and excellent dining options.

I borrowed a car from my cousin, and the three of us started our journey to Tateshina, Nagano. We reached the hotel in approximately an hour, and my mother was very excited when we arrived. This was her first experience visiting a hot spring.

When it came time to enjoy the hot spring baths, Kris gave my mother the extra one-piece bathing suit she had packed specifically for her. The swim suit was far too big on my diminutive mother, but it did the trick.

The highlight of our visit was the dinner. We gathered in a huge dining room along with the other onsen guests, and a lavish buffet was spread out before us. My mother was like a little kid in a candy store. I do not think she had ever eaten many of the items she enjoyed that night. We had a selection of crab legs, well-prepared sushi, roast beef, side dishes of various types, and mouth-watering desserts. Kris and I were really happy that she enjoyed this trip. She talked about it incessantly with the neighbors when we returned.

My Proposal to Kris

After living together for four years, Kris reminded me that it was time to take our relationship to the next level. I agreed that the time had come for me to formally propose to her, but it was going to be done in my own unique way. I decided to propose using the technology that was available to me.

I propped up my cell phone on my desk and set it to record my message to Kris. I selected a song that was appropriate for the occasion, "A Time for Us" by Andy Williams. I dressed in a nice suit, but I looked too ordinary. I enhanced my outfit with a hair band and a yellow rose tucked in it. I attached a roach clip with blue feathers hanging down to my right ear lobe. In place of a tie, I wore a giant bright pink gift ribbon I had purchased from the Dollar Tree store. Finally, I pulled it all together with a pair of aviator sunglasses. The sunglasses were to disguise the fact that

I was reading the proposal I had written on a piece of paper attached to my desktop computer screen. The only unfortunate thing was that I had a huge cold sore on my lip.

I hit the record button on my cell phone. With Andy Williams singing in the background, I said the following words to Kris:

Hello, Kris! There is a nice song playing in the background, "A Time for Us," the love theme from Romeo and Juliette by Andy Williams.

It's been four years since we started living together, and we've had a lot of fun. It's been smooth sailing, and it's time for us to move one step forward.

You know I am not the average Joe, and I do a lot of things in different ways. When it comes to a marriage proposal, it is not an exception.

I did not hire an airplane to write out a proposal in the sky. I did not ask a TV station to give me a chance to propose to you on the air. I did not plan an elaborate scheme to do the job.

I am simply using this sophisticated media technology to accomplish the task. The end result will be the same. I have not gotten the ring yet, because I want to get you the ring that you want. So, I want to go wedding ring shopping with you this weekend.

So, please marry me! Please! Please!

When she came home, I played the video for her. She laughed, cried, and said yes.

Married in Las Vegas

We decided to get married in Las Vegas and selected October 4, 2011 as our wedding date. Since we had both been married before, we did not want an elaborate wedding with a lot of guests. We found a wedding coordinator in Las Vegas who arranged everything for us.

We arrived at South Point Hotel Casino & Spa in Las Vegas on October 2. The next day, we visited the Clark County Marriage License Bureau to obtain our marriage license and met with our wedding coordinator. On the day of our wedding, we were picked up at the hotel by a limousine and taken to the wedding venue. It was enjoyable to walk through the casino in the hotel lobby wearing our wedding attire.

When we arrived at the venue, we were met by the wedding coordinator, officiant, and photographer. Our ceremony was performed at Heritage Garden in Lakeside Village. It rained on the day of our wedding, and we were a little concerned about having the ceremony take place outdoors, but everything went smoothly. The only hiccup happened during our vows when I asked the officiant to repeat what she said, as I had a hard time hearing her.

After returning to Redondo Beach, we flew to Honolulu for our honeymoon. I was a little apprehensive about going to Hawaii on our honeymoon since I had gone there on my previous two honeymoons and those marriages had failed. Kris knew that she would be my third wife, and my father had been married four times. At this point, I have no intention of tying his marriage record or surpassing it.

My first wife and I are on good terms since we have two children together. When Kris and I travel north to see my daughters during the holidays, we all have our holiday dinner together.

Dabbling in YouTube

With the pervasiveness of various sharing platforms, people's hobbies and jobs have changed to keep up with the technology. In the 1970s, influencers consisted of a group of iconic individuals such as Cher, Diana Ross, Farrah Fawcett, Liza Minelli, and Olivia Newton-John. Today, thanks to YouTube, just about anyone can be an influencer if they create content that gathers a large following.

I am by no means an influencer, but I do maintain my own YouTube channel. I started out by lip-synching to various songs by popular singers like Bette Midler and Kiyohiko Ozaki. Later, I started to upload videos of me playing guitar. You can find a series of QR codes in Appendix A for the various YouTube videos I have created over the years.

My Mother Adopted my Cousin's Daughter

Before my father passed away, he entered into an agreement with my cousin to adopt one of his children. My cousin had one son and two daughters, and since my parents had no hope of me returning to Japan, my cousin obliged. Unfortunately, the adoption did not take place while my father was still alive.

My cousin sent his youngest daughter, Masuko, to art college, and she had strong aspirations of becoming an artist. However, since my cousin wanted to honor the agreement he had made with my father, he allowed my mother to adopt Masuko. Masuko was against being adopted by my mother, but she could not go against her father's wishes. In 2013, when my mother was 90 years old, the adoption was made legal and Masuko went to live with my mother.

At the time, my mother seemed to be suffering from Alzheimer's disease. Since no one really knew about it, her relationship with Masuko got off to a rocky start. As is typical of an Alzheimer's patient, she was paranoid and accused Masuko of hiding and stealing her belongings.

I called her every weekend, and she incessantly complained about my adopted sister. I did my best to calm the situation down, but with my mother's consent we all eventually agreed to send my mother to an adult daycare facility. At first, it was just a couple of days a week, and eventually grew to one week at a time. My mother never complained about spending longer periods of time at the facility.

While she was at the adult daycare, she was diagnosed with mid-stage Alzheimer's disease. Then we realized we should have recognized the signs when she was not getting along well with Masuko, and we should have taken better care of her.

Even though my mother was progressively growing weaker physically, she always had a good appetite.

Keeping My Brain Active

In 2014, I began to sense that my brain was not as sharp as when I was in my twenties. I started to experience problems with my memory. To keep my brain active, I decided to take up Spanish, even though I had taken one semester of Spanish at a local junior college earlier.

I purchased a 300-page Spanish lesson book from the bookstore and began to study it on my own. I spent at least one hour a day studying the book, and within six months I managed to finish it. However, I kept going back to the book because I had trouble retaining what I had learned. In four years' time, I went over the entire book three times, which really frustrated me. Even now, I occasionally browse through the book's pages.

My wife is greatly interested in Japanese language and culture, so we often watch Japanese TV programs together while I act as a translator. Sometimes, instead of translating the Japanese into English, I translate it into Spanish for a fun, which seems to frustrate her.

Another way I keep my brain active is by playing electric guitar. Although I knew how to play acoustic guitar, playing electric guitar was new to me. I don't consider myself a musically talented person, and my acoustic guitar playing is only at the intermediate level. Due to my hearing problems, my singing is even worse, although I love to sing.

At our neighborhood Guitar Center, I purchased an electric guitar, an amplifier, and other small, related items for under $800. I really loved the sounds my new electric guitar produced, and I launched into learning to play new songs.

When I listened to "Canon Rock" by Jerry C for the first time, I fell in love with it. I obtained the music and attempted to learn to play the five-minute, 43-second piece. Although I could read music, I found this piece very challenging to learn. But once I am determined to do something, nothing can stop me. I even went to a guitar school four times to get the hang of it. However, after spending hours and hours learning how to master the music, I finally gave up. I was told later that Canon Rock is an extremely difficult piece for a beginner to learn. I eventually moved on to play slower and much easier pieces.

In June 2022, my older daughter, Ann, got married. Three months before her wedding, I had decided to play a Japanese song at her wedding. I did not want to embarrass Ann or myself, so I spent at least two hours every day working to master the piece. In the course of learning how to play it, I became very frustrated because my fingers and brain did not coordinate well. There were times when I forgot where to place my fingers on the frets. The only way for me to learn this song was by repeating it over and over again, until muscle memory moved my fingers where they needed to be without relying on my brain's instructions.

My efforts paid off, and my guitar performance was flawless during the wedding. My wife videotaped my performance and uploaded it on YouTube. The QR code for that recording is included in Appendix A as well.

Unfortunately, all of that practicing created stiffness on the left side of my neck and shoulder. My orthopedic doctor told me I had developed arthritis on the left side of my neck. I do not regret it because I flawlessly played the music that I wanted to play for my daughter on her wedding day. I still play my electric guitar occasionally, despite my arthritis.

Bessho Onsen, Ueda City

Since my mother had enjoyed her first trip to an onsen in 2010, we decided to invite her to accompany us to an even nicer onsen facility in 2016.

Nanakusa No Yu Ryokan in Bessho Onsen, Ueda City, was about an hour and a half away by car. I rented a car because the truck I borrowed from my mother to drive around town during our previous visits could not accommodate the three of us and had no air conditioning.

I have to say that I did enjoy driving that little truck as it provided the perfect driving position for me. Also, that little truck could easily attain speeds of 50 miles per hour. I once drove it on the curving, mountain roads at high speeds, drifting around the corners. My wife, who was sitting in the passenger seat, enjoyed the drive as much as I did. She is as much a thrill seeker as I am, and she does not get scared easily.

When the three of us arrived at the onsen, we were greeted by the owner and led to our room. It had its own private onsen tub overlooking the Bessho valley. Breakfast and dinner were brought to our room, and my mother was very impressed with the food and service. This onsen was much more expensive than the previous one, but it was worth it to see her fully enjoying herself. It was a small way for me to thank her for all that she had done for me over the years.

After we returned to the U.S., my adopted sister told me that my mother kept talking about the exciting experiences at the hotel.

xxiv. With my mother at Bessho Onsen

xxv. My mother's truck, Nagano, Japan

Corvette Fever

I have always had a fascination with cars, and I have owned many makes and models in my lifetime. (Please see the list provided in Appendix B). I had owned three Chevy Corvettes, but I was extremely impressed with the 2017 model's styling and performance. I had to have it. I was interested in the white Grand Sport (C7), and after some online research, I located a dealer who had the car in their lot.

My wife and I drove to the dealership to pick up the car. I was in seventh heaven while driving it home. The car was very fast and very loud. If I started the engine early in the morning with the garage door open, the sound rattled the walls and woke up the entire neighborhood.

Soon, taking the Corvette on the scenic Highway 1 along the ocean became our favorite weekend activity. We took the thirty-mile round trip once every weekend. When we reached the halfway point, I made a U-turn and ensured that there were no cars behind us. Then I pushed the accelerator pedal to the floor until the speedometer registered 80 miles per hour while my wife screamed with joy in the passenger seat. We both enjoyed the amazing acceleration of the C7. We repeated this stunt weekly for nineteen months, and I am sure we irritated those who lived along the road.

I sold the Corvette after enjoying it for nineteen months, although I had only driven it 2,200 miles in that time. I lost $15,000 when I sold the car, but owning it gave me an opportunity of a lifetime. I participated in the Ron Fellows Performance Driving School three-day event near Las Vegas.

I paid $1,000, which was a discounted price for new Corvette owners. The event included free lodging, breakfast, and lunch for two days for me and my wife. We arrived at the school in January 2018, and it rained the entire time. Nonetheless, the event went on as scheduled.

xxvi. My 2017 Corvette

The facility was enormous and had several racing tracks as well as condominiums for the racing participants. Since the condominium units were fully booked, the school put us up at a nearby hotel. Each day, we were taught the basic racing skills using their new Corvettes. After the classroom instruction ended, we were assigned a car to drive while following our instructor. Sadly, due to the rain and the wet pavement, we could not drive the 2.2-mile course at full throttle as I wanted to.

xxvii. My 2020 Corvette

Despite this little setback, I really enjoyed the event. My wife got several chances to ride as a passenger in the instructor's car. Other drivers' wives became sick or scared after doing so, but my wife fully enjoyed the experience and eagerly repeated it over and over again. On our drive back home, we both had immense grins on our faces.

I enjoyed the driving school so much that I decided to do it again. However, this time I had to pay $3,500 for the same class. In June 2018, my wife and I drove to the facility again. This time, we were housed in one of the condominium units. The winds were really kicking up, and my

xxviii. At Ron Fellows Performance Driving School

wife had a severe allergy attack. She was forced to stay indoors and watch through the condominium window as I raced around the track. All three days were extremely hot, so we had to race with the air conditioning on. This time, I got to know the full potential of my 2017 Corvette Grand Sport.

In the summer of 2019, General Motors revealed the new 2020 Corvette Stingray (C8) that it was going to release. I loved its styling and performance as much as I loved those of the previous model (2017). In November 2020, I placed a $5,000 deposit on the car with the same dealership where I had purchased the 2017 model. Due to the supply chain problems created by the COVID-19 pandemic, I had to wait an entire year for my new car to be delivered to me.

As advertised, its performance was amazing. It was much quicker than the previous model. Like before, we drove it on our usual route along Highway 1 and pushed the gas pedal to the floor at the halfway point. I am sure that the people living near the half-way point lamented the fact that the crazy Corvette owner had returned.

Since the new Corvette entitled me to another opportunity to participate in the racing school for $1,000, I took it. This time, due to the COVID-19 pandemic, Kris did not come with me. Like before, I really enjoyed the school, but I felt that I could get better times when we were allowed to race solo with other student drivers. My best time then was 1 minute 54 seconds, which was not bad at all.

I sold the Corvette twelve months later for a profit of $15,000. I had put less than 2,000 miles on the car. You could say that I get tired of cars easily.

I was eager to further test my racing skills and inquired about participating in another course at the same driving school. Due to the COVID-19 pandemic the school did not have very many participants, so it offered me a two-day course scheduled to begin on November 25, 2021. I had the 2.2-mile course and instructor all to myself! The first day was dedicated to basic driving skills, as before, and the second day was dedicated to one-on-one driving instruction with the dedicated instructor. I only paid $3,500 for this experience and attained my best time of 1 minute and 51 seconds, which may rank among the top ten percent of the times attained by the student drivers. I was very happy that I had this opportunity.

xxix. With long, braided hair

xxx. With long hair tied back and yukata

My Mother Passed Away

My mother passed away on October 13, 2017, at the age of 94. That day also happened to be a Friday the thirteenth.

She had suffered from aspiration, a condition where food enters the lungs and causes pneumonia, for six months prior to her death. She was forced to receive her nourishment through an IV for three months.

Unfortunately, I was not at her bedside when she passed away. I was grateful for having had a few opportunities to thank her for taking care of me and helping me. That was something I could not do for my father before he passed away.

Before my mother was cremated, we had a funeral at her house with about twenty people in attendance. It is highly unusual for anyone to make a long speech at a funeral in Japan, but that did not deter me. I read the following letter over my mother's body as it lay in the casket.

> *Although the duration of my mother's disease was relatively short, I would like to express my gratitude to my immediate family members and other relatives for compassionately caring for my mother.*
>
> *Before I embarked on my trip to Japan to attend this funeral, my eldest daughter, Ann, said to me, "Grandma was an amazing person. She was tough, and she was always working hard and striving for her goals. She taught me how important it is to work hard all the time." It is true that like my mother, Ann had worked hard. She had a full-time job and studied for three years to obtain her PhD in kinesiology. When I told my mother about Ann's accomplishment, she was*

extremely happy about it, just as if she had received the degree herself.

According to my mother, when she was small, she endured hard times since her father, my grandfather, lost a lot of money in commodities and antiques. During World War II, she worked at a cotton mill in Nagoya. After the war ended, she found work in Tokyo as a house maid working for a wealthy family. However, after six months, she was relieved of her duties due to food shortages in Tokyo, and she had no choice but to return to Nagano, where she found work in a blacksmith shop. She worked there until 1949, the year she married my father. Since she worked hard for the family in Tokyo and gained their trust, the head of that household sent gifts to my mother every year, and she reciprocated until the day he died.

Shortly after marrying my father, my older brother and I were born, and my mother worked very hard growing apples and rice from early in the morning until well into the evening hours. When I visited her about 20 years ago, I woke up for the bathroom around 4 o'clock in the morning and I saw a figure moving in the peach orchard. I was surprised to find that it was my mother who was already working.

When my brother was 13 and I was 11 years old, my brother died in a tragic accident. I cannot imagine what my mother went through after that and how difficult it must have been for her.

After graduating from high school, I left home to attend college near Tokyo. However, against my parents' strong objections, I quit college after two years and worked as a vacuum truck driver for nine months to save some money and attend a college in the U.S.

I obtained my Bachelor of Science degree in the U.S. after four and a half years while my parents fully supported me financially. To earn the money to send to me every three months, my mother started working in a small factory at the age of 52. She worked from 8 a.m. to 5 p.m., and she took care of her crops before and after her regular work hours. I was surprised by her toughness and determination.

After my graduation in 1977, I came back to Nagano and got a job at Tiyoda Manufacturing Company. After working there for two months, I realized that living in Japan was not for me, and I returned to the U.S. after having a huge fight with my parents. For almost a year and a half, I had not spoken to them. I felt very bad about having caused my mother so much emotional stress regarding my leaving Nagano for the U.S. To compensate for my bad behavior, since my father's death, I have been calling my mother at least once a week. Every time I came back to Nagano to see her, I asked her to go to an onsen with me, but she always refused. I believed that, in a way, it would have been a lot of trouble for her to go, but in actuality she really did not want her son to spend his money on her.

However, in 2010, my wife and I finally had the opportunity to take her to a nice onsen. In my eyes, she really enjoyed the onsen experience; it must have been a totally different world for her then. To me, she deserved this because she had worked hard all her life. She retired from taking care of her apple and peach orchards when she was 88 years old. I thought, "at least I was able to show my appreciation to her for helping me all her life."

Last year, my wife and I were able to take her to a much nicer onsen, and reserved the best room there, because she was already 93 years old and we did not know what the future would hold for her. I believe that she really enjoyed herself there. Even after we came back home, she kept talking about her experiences at the onsen. When we were ready to come back to the U.S., I thought this could be the last time I saw my mother, which unfortunately came true.

I did not have a chance to be by her bedside, which I do not regret. I knew she was gravely ill in the hospital, but I was hoping every day that she would not suffer since she had worked very hard all her life. And I did not want her to suffer any more when she died. I heard that three nurses were at her bedside when she passed away. I am glad she did not die alone. As she was dying, I was told that her breathing gradually decreased, and she passed away peacefully, which led me to believe that she probably did not suffer any pain.

Before my father died, I never had the opportunity to tell him how much I appreciated him for all he did for me. I have been regretting this ever since. As for my mother, I never wanted to repeat the same mistake, so about a year and a half ago, I had the courage to say, "Thank you, mother, for all you have done for me." This comment left her speechless as she never expected to hear such a comment coming from me. However, I believe that she got my message. So, I do not have any regret as far as my mother is concerned.

The following are the last words from me to you, mother. I fully appreciate you for raising and nurturing such a selfish and sometimes bad son. As for my long hair, you might say, "What a stupid hairstyle!" But this is the last time I will behave badly toward you before you cross over to a different world. So, please forgive me. I am going to bring your ashes back to the U.S. and combine them with my father's. I promise that I am going to pray to them every day.

Mother! You do not have to work hard anymore, and please rest in peace. Please protect me, the only remaining survivor of the original Ohkubo family.

Isshuki: First Anniversary of my Mother's Death

2018 marked the first anniversary of my mother's death. Kris and I traveled to Nagano that year to attend the ceremony held at the temple. We stayed at my adopted sister Masuko's house for a few days. Masuko got married in 2015. She and her husband now live in my mother's old house with their two children, aged four and seven.

Due to her father-in-law's insistence, Masuko changed her maiden name of Ohkubo to her husband's surname, Tsukada. She gave up on the idea of becoming an artist and currently devotes her time to taking care of her two children full-time. Her husband, with whom I get along fine, works for a roofing company.

After the ceremony concluded, Kris and I bid farewell to our relatives in Nagano and embarked on the sightseeing portion of our trip to visit Kanazawa, Kyoto, Nara, and Osaka. In Kyoto, for the sake of convenience, we joined a tour group and visited some historical landmarks, including those in Nara, by tour bus. In Osaka, we met up with my old friend and former roommate from San Luis Obispo, Takada-kun. He drove us around, and we enjoyed *yakiniku* (grilled meat) in Dotonbori together. The area running along the Dotonbori canal is known to be one of the principal tourist destinations in Osaka. After parting from Takada-kun, we toured the rest of Osaka on our own.

The next morning, we boarded a bullet train at the Osaka station bound for Tokyo, where we stayed at our usual hotel, Hotel Ryumeikan near the Tokyo station, for two nights before returning to the U.S.

While in Tokyo, we visited Odaiba, a popular shopping and entertainment destination located on a man-made island in Tokyo Bay. On our last night in Tokyo, we gathered with five of my old friends from San Luis Obispo to have dinner and drinks at a very nice restaurant near the Tokyo station. For a few short hours, we enjoyed recalling all of our good, bad, and crazy times together in SLO. One of the five friends is Ryu-kun, whom I did not mention before. He is the son of the most famous Enka singer in Japan, Kitajima Saburo. Saburo-san was the owner of a very prestigious thoroughbred racehorse known as Kitasan Black. In his three-year track career, he won twelve of his twenty races, including seven Grade 1 events, four JRA awards, and set the record for the most prize money won in Japan. Ryu-kun gifted us with a bottle of sake that was specifically made to commemorate the horse's most recent win.

Helping My Kids

I always tell my wife that I want to help my kids the same way my parents helped me. In August 2020, I purchased my second townhouse in Rohnert

Park, California. I bought the property so my younger daughter, Lynn, a divorcee, could live there comfortably with her three children.

xxxi. Ohkubo family reunion buttons

Ohkubo Family Reunion in Hawaii

My oldest daughter, Ann, had plans to honeymoon in Honolulu after her wedding in June 2022. Since the COVID-19 pandemic prevented us from getting together for the holidays as we usually do, we decided that this would be a good time for all of us to get together in Hawaii. Thus, the idea of an Ohkubo family reunion was born.

Ten family members and a friend with her daughter, all originating from different parts of California, boarded planes bound for Daniel K. Inouye

International Airport in Honolulu in July 2022. Imagine! Fifty-one years ago, I arrived in California, alone, to attend school. Now, there are ten of us. Our group included my current wife, Kris, and me; my first wife, Alice (the mother of my children, who still uses the surname Ohkubo); my daughter Ann, her wife Aubree, and their son Kenichi; my daughter Lynn, and her three children, Brent, Jessica, and Mia; and Lynn's former sister-in-law and her daughter. We had special reunion badges made for everyone to wear.

Kris and I stayed in our usual hotel on Waikiki Beach, and everyone else shared a huge two-bedroom suite at Disney's Aulani Resort. We enjoyed various activities as a family and separately, and we had an amazing time.

Semi-Retired Life

Most people living in Japan never retire. They simply start new careers when they reach retirement age, which is known as "a second life." Since I own my own business, which is more like a hobby to me. So I suppose I will never actually retire.

But one thing I do enjoy at this later age is my hobbies, which range from attending sporting events to gardening.

Kris and I are avid sports fans, and we love cheering on our favorite teams. We are devoted to the Los Angeles Angels baseball team and the Los Angeles Clippers basketball team. Neither of us really cares for the Dodgers or the Lakers, so we don't have a rivalry with one another when it comes to sports. We also love supporting underdogs.

Prior to the COVID-19 pandemic, we attended sporting events several times each year. We were fortunate enough to see up close baseball's two-way sensation from Japan, Shohei Ohtani, several times. We are both looking forward to attending the basketball games at the Clippers' new, state-of-the-art stadium in 2024.

It may seem preposterous for someone who behaved the way I did when I was younger to have a hobby raising Monarch butterflies, but I assure you that it is quite true.

The whole thing came about accidentally. Seven years ago, when I was working in my patio garden, I came across a plant I did not recognize. Its leaves were unusually foul-smelling, but it had delicate red and orange flowers. I searched the internet to determine what type of plant it was and learned that it was a perennial plant called milkweed. I also learned that the milkweed is the only host plant for monarch butterflies. Monarch caterpillars feed exclusively on its leaves; therefore, the plant plays an essential role in the monarch's life cycle.

I allowed the plant to grow in my garden, and when it had reached a height of a little over two feet, I saw a few small caterpillars, barely half an inch in length, crawling on its leaves. I took the caterpillars inside and placed them inside clear plastic containers, one caterpillar per container. I fed them the leaves from the milkweed plant and watched them grow. The transformation of the monarchs from tiny caterpillars to cocoons and finally to iconic butterflies was truly amazing. I became determined to raise monarchs from that point on.

xxxii. One of the monarchs from the Ohkubo Monarch Farm

I believe that in a period of seven years, I have raised over 300 monarchs from caterpillars to butterflies and released them out into the environment. I started out with a single milkweed plant, and now I have nine of them planted in flower pots out in my patio garden.

I never wanted to follow in my parents' footsteps and become a farmer, but gardening in my small patio garden gives me great satisfaction. I seem to have inherited my mother's green thumb.

A few years ago, I planted over fifteen cosmos plants, which remind me of my parents' property in Nagano. The average height for these annual plants with colorful, daisy-like flowers is one to four feet. My plants sprang to a height of over eight feet! They were out of control. Last year, I wanted to avoid the cosmos takeover and planted fifty zinnia plants instead. They turned out to be very hearty and bloomed constantly for almost three months. Growing things seems to be a part of my genetic makeup.

I have always been good with my hands, and I enjoy fixing things around the house. I have done nearly all of the plumbing and electrical work myself. I enjoy taking on various projects such as painting, replacing the bathroom floors, refinishing the cabinets, and laying concrete. My wife never gives me a "honey do" list.

Although I own an acoustic guitar, I seldom play it these days. In the past, I generally devoted at least two hours a day to practicing my electric guitar. However, my arthritis has forced me to reduce my practice time to less than fifteen minutes a day.

When I am not gardening or playing my guitar, I play shogi online to stimulate my brain. I do not play as often as I did in the past, but I still manage to squeeze in a few games on a daily basis.

As a youngster, I had an insatiable interest in space. That enthusiasm only grew stronger when I became an adult. I love reading about space exploration, how the universe was formed, and other related topics. The launch of the Hubble Space Telescope opened up a new world of discovery, and I keep up-to-date on all space-related news.

Throughout my life, I was never really involved in politics. I identify myself as a Democrat and carry out my civic duties by voting when called to do so. However, since Donald Trump became the 45th president of the United States, I have been involved in politics more than usual.

After a series of back and neck problems, I basically gave up going to the gym. I was always the type of person who trained his body and kept himself physically fit, so this setback was very frustrating for me. However, I do not plan to let this deter me. I push myself to walk several miles a day, five days a week. As Clint Eastwood once said, "I get up every day and don't let the old man in."

Of course, cars are my perpetual hobby. I currently subscribe to various auto-related newsletters to keep up on the latest news and trends. I handle the vehicle maintenance for our two cars, as well as all of the vehicles owned by my daughters and their families.

I no longer compete in autocross, but Kris and I enjoy attending drag racing events in Pomona together. Ever since we began dating, and throughout our married life, we have attended countless auto shows and events. My dream is to return to the Ron Fellows Corvette Racing School at least once more in my lifetime.

Before I married Kris, I had not been much of a traveler. I traveled out of necessity rather than for pleasure. Kris changed that and helped me enjoy traveling more. Our future travel plans include jaunts to our best-loved destinations, including Las Vegas, Japan, and Hawaii. We would like to visit Europe too, especially Spain, so I can practice my Spanish.

Too Much Time on My Hands

The big advantage that comes from being semi-retired is that I have more free time than I know what to do with. I have always enjoyed helping people, and now I can devote more time to that particular task.

Over the years, I have supplemented my knowledge and years of experience with extensive internet research to help others with various medical and legal (not criminal) issues.

For example, the knowledge I gained from my own experiences with immigration allowed me to help another individual with this dilemma. I was asked to look after a Japanese friend's son while he was attending a community college in California on a student (F1) visa. One summer, he returned to Japan during summer break to see his parents. When he returned to Los Angeles, he evidently falsified some information on his immigration document. I no longer recall the specifics of the case, but he was immediately deported back to Japan as a result.

I had gone to the airport to pick him up, but he never exited the airport. I found out, hours later, that he had been deported. Both he and his father were devastated by what had transpired, and his father asked me to help his son return to the U.S. At the time, I was told that if an individual was deported, he or she would not be permitted to return to the U.S. for a period of ten years following the deportation.

Although it was a monumental task to tackle, I decided to accept the challenge and help my friend and his son. At that time, the internet was still in its infancy, but I did all I could to research various ways to handle this case. Based on my research, I prepared numerous documents to submit to the immigration office on behalf of my friend's son. Then, it occurred to me that it might be better if an immigration attorney's name appeared on the paperwork. I hired a third-rate immigration lawyer who basically just submitted the documents that I prepared.

Luckily, my friend's son won a green card lottery. In three months, the deportation was reversed and my friend's son was granted legal alien status (he became a green card holder). I spent countless hours on this project, and although I had no intention of asking for compensation, my friend gave me $400 during our next meeting.

Seeing his son's happy face when I picked him up at Los Angeles International Airport gave me a great sense of accomplishment. Ultimately, he did not continue his education at the community college and found a job at a local sushi restaurant instead. He became a sushi chef and has been working in a sushi restaurant in central California for over 25 years now. He is married and the father of two children. I am truly glad that I was able to help change someone's life for the better.

Dabbling in California Law

As I wrote earlier, I am afforded a sufficient amount of free time as a semi-retired individual. I take full advantage of it and use my free time in a manner which benefits others. If you read this far in the book, you might have concluded that I do enjoy helping people. In fact, no request is too challenging or too time consuming. I always dedicate myself to the cause.

Having said that, I have engaged in matters involving California family law. I have helped friends with such matters as the dissolution of marriage, child custody, child support, spousal support, and drafting a prenuptial agreement. I am a diligent researcher and very adept at preparing legal documents. For example, when I helped a friend file for bankruptcy, I prepared over twenty pages of legal documents for the case. Assisting with the prenuptial agreement involved drafting a twenty-five-page document, which required many hours of research and preparation. All my hard work did pay off, however, and saved my friend both time and thousands of dollars in attorney fees. The only thing he needed to do was to hire an attorney to review my draft. With a few minor modifications, the document was easily accepted by my friend's partner's counsel.

With the uncertainties brought on by the COVID-19 pandemic, Kris and I decided to prepare a revocable living trust in 2021. Before we began the process of screening lawyers to handle the matter, I spent countless hours on the internet educating myself on the subject. It was a very complex trust, and the first few attorneys we interviewed wanted to charge exorbitant fees to prepare our documents. We finally found a local attorney who was willing to work on our trust for almost half the fee the others wanted to charge.

However, I believe that he underestimated the work involved since the distribution of our estate is a lot more involved and complicated than it initially seemed. I decided to take the matter into my own hands to avoid having to pay the attorney the hourly fees necessary to handle the extra work. I drafted the document pertaining to the distribution of our estate. It was so complicated that I had to prepare a flowchart so our lawyer would have a clear understanding of what we were trying to do. Ultimately, our trust document grew to seventy pages, not including the supporting documents, and it took over three months to complete the work. I was responsible for drafting twenty pages of that document. In doing so, I ensured that we did not spend a penny over what we were initially quoted by the law office.

I applied the same diligence to projects involving insurance claims. Whether it was a personal liability claim or an auto accident, I always meticulously prepared all of the necessary documentation to help support our case. Each time, those I have assisted, and even myself on occasion, received exactly what we were entitled to receive—and nothing less.

Being a Hypochondriac

As I age, I have become more sensitive about my well-being. While I understand that aches and pains come with age, I find it hard to accept. Any discomfort I experience causes great concern to me, and I seek medical advice right away. Fortunately, my wife's medical insurance covers these frequent doctor visits.

I typically do not bother with a primary care physician because in all likelihood he or she would send me to a specialist anyway. Instead, I have accumulated thirty-five specialists over the years who have treated me for various ailments or have addressed my concerns.

The thoroughness and diligence that I mentioned before also carries over to these doctor visits. I always bring a sheet of paper with me detailing my symptoms to every consultation. I do this because my memory is not as reliable as it used to be, and I do not want to leave anything out when I speak with my doctor. Although many doctors do not even bother to read what I have written, there are some who appreciate my thoroughness and devotion to my own healthcare.

One of those doctors is my pain management specialist. Whenever I bring some paperwork with me, he asks what I brought and whether he can see it. When an MRI is involved, I thoroughly study the radiologist's report and MRI images before seeing my doctor. We review the MRI images together in his office, and my comments to him usually go something like this. "I believe I have developed arthritis in my neck. Look at C5/C6. There is facet hypotrophy there causing my neck and shoulder pain. Can you try a cervical medial branch block to make sure that my assessment is correct? If it works, can you try an RFA (radiofrequency ablation) procedure?"

On the other hand, this does not work with my orthopedic doctor, who has very little tolerance for my know-it-all attitude. I saw him three times for the same issue, and each time he got upset and told me, "Mickey! I am your doctor, and you have to listen to me!"

During my third visit, he got so upset with me that he wanted to embarrass me in front of his female assistant. He sarcastically asked me what the term foramen means. Of course, I left him speechless by correctly answering his question using medical terminology. I was rather pleased with myself and thought, "Yes! He cannot give me shit like that since I am a seasoned internet doctor!"

But not all doctors are incapable of humoring a patient like me. Fifteen years ago, I had an orthopedic doctor whom I saw quite often. As soon as he opened the examination room door and saw me sitting there, he immediately closed the door. When he entered the room, he said, "Why me? What now?"

Normally, after I explained my situation to him, he agreed with my assessment and accommodated my needs. Once, I jokingly asked him if he had samples of Viagra, which he did. And he was willing to give me some, just to keep me happy.

Over the years, I have referred my wife to some of these doctors. As soon as they learned that she was my wife, they all inquired how she copes with such a crazy man. Lately, when she visits any of my specialists, she withholds the fact that we are married in an effort to avoid the embarrassment.

Still Crazy After All These Years

Takada-kun, my old friend and former roommate from my San Luis Obispo days, decided to come to the U.S. to watch Shohei Ohtani play for the Los Angeles Angels at Angels Stadium. I surprised him on his honeymoon by hiding in the bed at Madonna Inn.

When I learned of his visit, I told him that he could stay at my place. Despite being forewarned by our other SLO friends that he might be pranked, he accepted my offer. After all, we were roommates, and he was well aware of my bizarre sense of humor.

He arrived on May 19, 2023, and I picked him at Los Angeles International Airport. The following day, my wife and I drove him to San Luis Obispo to visit his alma mater, Cuesta College. We also stopped off at our old stomping grounds in Morro Bay and Cal Poly. We capped the day off by enjoying a meal at Louisa's Place, where I had worked as a dishwasher back in 1978. The restaurant was still there after all these years, albeit under new management. Best of all, Takada-kun thoroughly enjoyed his stroll down memory lane.

On May 21, we drove down to Anaheim to see Ohtani pitch. Takada-kun was thrilled to see the star athlete pitch live, and when the Angels won the game, it was the icing on the cake for us. On the 22nd, since my wife had to work, Takada-kun and I spent a quiet and uneventful day together. We visited Hermosa Beach, where we rented a couple of beach cruisers. We rode our bikes on The Strand, a 22-mile paved walkway that runs along the shoreline. Takada-kun was surprised by how wide and far our California beaches stretch. After all, the entire country of Japan can easily fit inside the state of California.

I refused to pull any pranks on Takada-kun for the first three days, as I believed that he might have his guard up. However, on the fourth day, the moment finally arrived. I set my alarm clock to wake me up at 3 a.m. Even though Takada-kun is a deep sleeper, I quietly slipped into the bathroom and dressed myself to resemble a traditional Japanese ghost.

I combed my long black hair over my face and fashioned a *tenkan* (a small, white triangular piece of cloth typically displayed on the forehead) out of a piece of white paper. I put on my *yukata* (a cotton summer kimono robe) and secured the tenkan on my forehead with a hairband.

With a flashlight in one hand and my cell phone in another, I slowly approached Takada-kun, who was fast asleep in the bed. I set my cell phone on video mode, ready to capture the moment. I turned on the flashlight and placed it under my chin to give my face an eerie, otherworldly glow. I poked him to wake him up, but he did not respond. He was in such a deep sleep that it took ten seconds to rouse him.

When he did wake and see my face, he let out a scream. "You scared the hell out of me!" Mission accomplished. He did not get angry with me since he expected to be pranked.

Needless to say, I was not satisfied with just one prank. My daughters had given me a gag gift for Christmas. It was a small spray bottle labeled "Wet Farts — Unleash a potent stench that will make your victims cry for fresh air!" I had tested it once and the stench was truly overwhelming. I do not believe that I had ever smelled anything quite as bad, even as a vacuum truck driver. It was the smell from hell.

Takada-kun was jet-lagged and napping on the bed. I thought the time was right to pull another prank on him. I went into the bathroom and, while holding my breath, thoroughly drenched a piece of paper towel with the Wet Farts spray. I walked over to where Takada-kun was sleeping and gently placed the wet paper towel under his nose. He woke up puzzled and did not know why I woke him up. I asked him if he smelled anything, and he responded, "No, my nose is stuffed up!"

Disappointed, I quickly placed the paper towel inside a plastic bag, sealed it, and put the bag inside the trash can. However, even though I acted swiftly, the damage was already done. My prank backfired on me. The smell made me gag several times, and I almost threw up. I had to exit the room immediately and could not return for the next couple of hours. Takada-kun, on the other hand, acted like nothing ever happened.

The following day, our friendship unaffected by my pranks, we went to see another Angels' game. Takada-kun left for Japan on May 24.

When I spoke with my SLO friends in Japan, I told them about what I had done to Takada-kun. Several of them told me that they did not have enough courage to stay with me at my place when they visit California in the future.

My pranking may have slowed down in my senior years, but the prankster in me is not dead yet. Every day is a new opportunity. Stay tuned!

xxxiii. Pranking Takada-kun in 2023

Appendices

Appendix A Links to My YouTube Channel

"I Started a Joke" by the Bee Gees

Mickey's musical performance during the wedding (2022)

Mickey's solo electric guitar playing "La Playa"

A Spanish song with 15 million hits

Mickey's electric guitar solo, "Blue Star" (1960)

Kiyohiko Ozaki, lip-synching

Koji Hirata, "Bus Stop" with Mickey Ohkubo

Shigeru Matsuzaki/ "Memory of Hage"

Bette Midler's "Wind Beneath My Wings," lip-synching

Appendix B Cars I Owned

1965 Corvette
1965 Pontiac Catalina
1965 Bradley GT (*A kit car*)
1965 Chevy Impala SS
1966 Corvette fastback
1966 Mustang 289
1968 Mustang fastback
1968 AMC Javelin
1968 AMC AMX
1968 Datsun 1600 roadster
1968 VW fastback
1968 Datsun 510
1968 Triumph TR250
1969 Datsun 2000 roadster
1970 Datsun pickup truck with a camper shell
1970 Datsun 510
1970 Triumph Spitfire
1973 Datsun 240Z
1973 Cadillac Sedan de Ville
1974 Fiat X19
1974 BMW Bavaria
1975 Porsche 911 Targa
1975 Audi
1975 VW Rabbit
1975 Datsun B210
1975 Ford Granada
1975 Honda Accord
1976 Nissan New Silvia
1976 Datsun 260Z
1977 Mazda RX 7
1978 Chevy Chevette
1978 Datsun 280Z
1978 Pontiac Tran Am
1979 Porsche 911 slant nose
1979 Lotus Esprit

1979 Corvette Stingray
1979 Jaguar XJS V12
1983 Cadillac Seville
1984 Fiero
1984 Mercedes 380SL
1985 Toyota Camry V6, leased
1985 Chevy IROC Z28
1986 Isuzu Impulse
1987 Toyota Supra
1987 Toyota Cressida
1988 Toyota Supra Turbo
1990 Lexus 400
1990 Toyota Camry
1993 Mazda RX7 (twin turbo)
1997 Ford Taurus

2004 Nissan 350Z (new)
2013 Toyota Avalon (new)
2017 Corvette Grand Sport (new)
2020 Corvette Stingray (new)[3]

---

[3] The list includes only the cars I owned for at least three months.

Appendix C Photos

i. Masayuki Ohkubo, Nagano, Japan iv
ii. My father, Takeshi 11
iii. My mother, Seki, my older brother, Yukio, and me 12
iv. A light blue Mazda 360 Coupe, similar to my car, auto show in Los Angeles 35
v. My boarding house in Saitama 41
vi. With friends in London (I'm in the middle) 61
vii. Carolyn and Richard 62
viii. On vacation in Mendocino County 62
ix. My Coming of Age ceremony outfit, Nagano, Japan 69
x. With one of my motorcycles, Nagano 70
xi. Circa 1973 84
xii. Photo taken by Akira 109
xiii. Circa 1977 124
xiv. Graduation photo 138
xv. With my parents, circa 1977 144
xvi. On the race course with the New Silvia 177
xvii. Kris and I on our wedding day, Las Vegas (October 4, 2011) 184
xviii. With my 1979 Porsche 911 (Slant Nose), circa 1992 206
xix. Aboard the Battleship USS Iowa in San Pedro, California 207
xx. My 2004 Nissan 350Z 235
xxi. Ueno Park, Japan 241
xxii. Kris's Christmas slippers 246
xxiii. The matching vest 248
xxiv. With my mother at Bessho Onsen 261
xxv. My mother's truck, Nagano, Japan 262
xxvi. My 2017 Corvette 264
xxvii. My 2020 Corvette 265
xxviii. At Ron Fellows Performance Driving School 266
xxix. With long, braided hair 268
xxx. With long hair tied back and yukata 269
xxxi. Ohkubo family reunion buttons 276

xxxii. One of the monarchs from the Ohkubo Monarch Farm 279
xxxiii. Pranking Takada-kun in 2023 291

Works Cited

Afshar, Dave. "Stereotypes All Japanese People Hate." Culture Trip, The Culture Trip, 23 Jan. 2017, https://theculturetrip.com/asia/japan/articles/15-stereotypes-all-japanese-people-hate/.

"Occupation of Japan." Wikipedia, Wikimedia Foundation, 17 Mar. 2023, https://en.wikipedia.org/wiki/Occupation_of_Japan.

www.ingramcontent.com/pod-product-compliance
Lightning Source LLC
Chambersburg PA
CBHW051543010526
44118CB00022B/2562